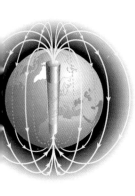

Tell Me
WHERE?

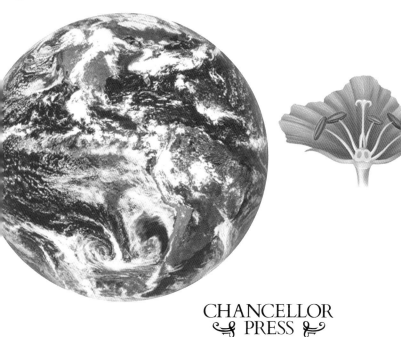
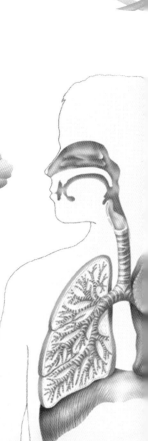

CHANCELLOR
PRESS

Jena Stewart

First published in 2002 by Chancellor Press,
an imprint of Octopus Publishing Group Ltd

Reprinted 2003 (twice), 2004 (three times), 2005 (three times),
2006 (three times), 2007 (twice), 2008, 2009 (twice)

New edition published in 2010 by Chancellor Press,
an imprint of Octopus Publishing Group Ltd,
189 Shaftesbury Avenue,
London WC2H 8JY
www.octopusbooks.co.uk

Reprinted 2011 (twice)

An Hachette UK Company
www.hachette.co.uk

ISBN: 978-0-753720-84-4

A CIP catalogue record for this book is available from the British Library

Produced by Omnipress, Eastbourne

Printed in China

CONTENTS

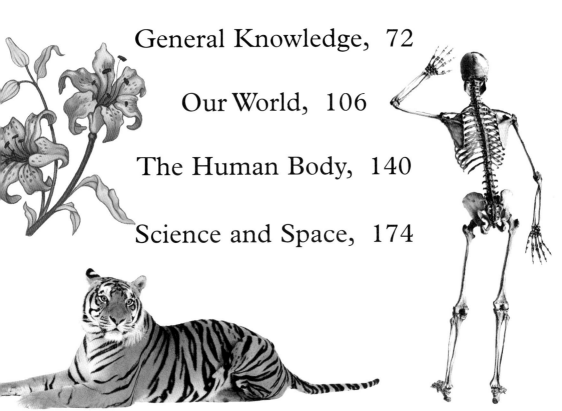

HISTORY
AND EVENTS

CONTENTS

· · · · · · · · · · · · · · · · · · · ·

WHERE DOES THE WORD 'HISTORY' COME FROM?

History comes from a Greek word meaning 'what is known by asking'. The job of a historian is to ask questions and make sense of the answers.

The Greeks were among the first people to write history based on first-hand reporting of the facts. Herodotus (who died in 425 BCE) wrote about the wars between the Greeks and the Persians. He travelled and talked to people who had taken part in the wars.

Historians work from a viewpoint. The first people to write their own history were the Chinese. We know the name of one early Chinese historian, Sima Qian, who wrote a history of China in about 100 BCE. Early historians felt it was important to write down the stories and legends of the past, and show how their state had come into existence. Sometimes

people who made history also wrote about it. Julius Caesar, the Roman general, wrote his own book about his campaigns in Gaul.

FACT FILE

The word 'archaeology' comes from two Greek words and means 'the study of old things'. Many archaeological discoveries are made by digging in the ground at sites where ancient people lived.

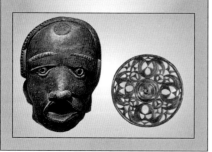

WHERE WOULD YOU HAVE SEEN A HOME OF MAMMOTH BONES?

Around 18,000 years ago, the last of a series of Ice Ages gripped much of the northern hemisphere. Icecaps spread southwards across Europe and North America. The sea level fell, uncovering land bridges which animals and people crossed – between Asia and Alaska for example.

Ice Age hunters, clothed only in animal skins, adapted to living in these freezing conditions. They built shelters from the bones of mammoths. They made the framework from the bones and filled in the gaps with skins, turf and moss. Groups of men drove the animals into swamps, where they became trapped and were killed with spears or rocks.

FACT FILE

Tools for scraping the skins of a hunted animal were made mostly from flint. This hard material could be chipped into tools of many different shapes and sizes. Other tools were made from bone, antlers and tusks.

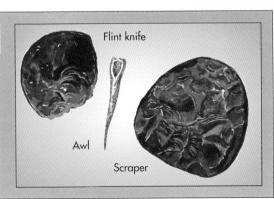

Flint knife

Awl

Scraper

WHERE WAS SUMER?

Mesopotamia, meaning 'between rivers', lay in the country we know as modern Iraq. Northern Mesopotamia's weather was mild, with enough rain for crops to grow in some areas. In the south lay a flat, swampy plain built up from mud spread by the river floodwaters. This area was called Sumer. It had little rain and long, hot summers. People had lived in Sumer since about 5000 BCE. They fished the rivers, hunted wild pigs and birds for food, and picked fruit from date palms. The muddy soil was rich, but crops died without rain in the burning summer heat so farmers dug canals to channel river water to their fields of barley, wheat, dates and vegetables. They turned over the earth with ploughs pulled by oxen.

Skilled metalworkers in Sumer made fine trinkets from silver and gold. These items were inlaid with precious stones, such as lapis lazuli.

Sumerian rob

Sumer body adornments

FACT FILE

Some of the wedge-shaped ('cuneiform') characters in the Sumerian writing system looked like objects, others were symbols.

WHERE DID SARGON OF AKKAD BUILD HIS EMPIRE?

Sargon of Akkad was a king who founded the first great empire in history. He built his empire in Mesopotamia (now mostly Iraq) in about 2300 BCE and gained control over much of southwestern Asia. Sargon was an outstanding military leader and administrator. He was one of the earliest kings to maintain a permanent army and to appoint associates from the royal court to serve as the governors of conquered cities. He organized his empire so well that it survived under his successors for over sixty years.

Sargon started his political career as cup-bearer to the king of Kish. Sargon later conquered Kish and the other Sumerian city states. Then he led his soldiers to a series of victories that extended his empire to what is now Iran in the east and to the Mediterranean Sea and Asia Minor (now Turkey) in the west. Sargon reigned for 56 years and built a magnificent capital city called Akkad.

FACT FILE

Sargon made one of his daughters a priestess of the moon god in Ur. The royal standard of Ur, a decorated wooden box, dates from about 2500 BC. On its mosaic panels, farmers parade and soldiers march into battle.

WHERE WAS THE WORLD'S FIRST GREAT CIVILIZATION?

The Indus Valley civilization was one of the world's first great societies. It developed out of farming and herding communities that carried on trade with each other. The civilization began to flourish about 4,500 years ago and was based in the vast river plains of what are now Pakistan and northwestern India. There were two main cities – Harappa in the north of the Indus Valley and Mohenjo Daro in the south. They were both carefully planned cities and laid out on a grid system. They had wide roads and brick houses, most of which had at least two storeys. Most homes had a bathing area that was supplied with water from a nearby public well or from a well in the courtyard of the house.

The people who lived there were farmers, tending to fields and watering crops with silt-laden waters washed down when the snows melted in the mountains to the north.

FACT FILE

The farmers of the Indus Valley used wooden carts pulled by a pair of oxen. Deep grooves made by heavily laden carts have been found in the excavated streets of Mohenjo Daro.

WHERE DID KING ASHURBANIPAL RULE?

From 668 to 627 BCE, Assyria, an ancient country on the upper Tigris River in Mesopotamia, was ruled by a king called Ashurbanipal. It covered roughly the northern part of present-day Iraq. Assyria's civilization was similar in many ways to that of ancient Babylon, which bordered it to the south. Ashurbanipal was the last great Assyrian ruler. He made the city of Nineveh his capital. Here he oversaw the building of a magnificent palace, a library and ornate gardens.

King Ashurbanipal

The Assyrian chief god was Assur, and the king was Assur's representative on Earth. The king was in charge of the army and the government, and he also controlled the temples and their priests.

Residents of some of the older cities, such as Assur and Nineveh, enjoyed special privileges, including low taxes and freedom from military service. Landlords had to pay taxes and provide young men from their estates to serve in the army. Beyond Assyria itself, the empire was divided into provinces. Each province was administered by a governor who was responsible to the central government.

FACT FILE

Assyrian artists made wall relief sculptures showing winged spirits, hunting scenes, lions and bulls. For sport, the Assyrian king and his nobles would kill captive lions released into special enclosures.

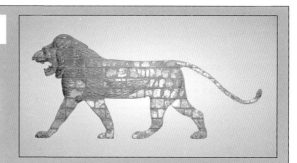

WHERE ARE THE RUINS OF PERSEPOLIS?

Persepolis was a capital of ancient Persia. King Darius I of Persia built Persepolis in about 500 BCE in a mountain region of what is now southwest Iran. Darius and his successors constructed large stone and mud-brick palaces in the capital, which became the royal ceremonial area for the religious holiday of the New Year. Every year at this festival, the king would renew his divine rights as king, and representatives of all the peoples within the Persian Empire would bring him gifts. In 330 BCE, Alexander the Great seized Persepolis.

Archaeologists have uncovered many of the ruins of Persepolis. Some of these ruins have been restored. Visitors may see a representation of the procession of New Year's gift givers carved in stone on two grand staircases leading to the king's audience hall.

FACT FILE

Ten thousand soldiers called the Immortals formed the core of the Persian army. Each spearman or archer was instantly replaced if killed.

WHERE WAS THE BATTLE OF SALAMIS?

Battle of Salamis

The Battle of Salamis took place on a Greek island of the same name, in the Saronic Gulf, about 16 km (10 miles) west of Athens. It covers 95 sq km (37 square miles) and much of the land is rocky, mountainous and lacking in vegetation. Because the island has an irregular crescent shape, Salamis is known as *Koulouri* which means 'baker's crescent'.

In 480 BCE the Greeks and Persians fought a great sea battle near Salamis. Arrows, stones and spears rained between the ships, but the Greek's key weapon was the ramming power of their galleys, driven at speed by banks of rowers. The Persian ships tried to block the advance of Greek vessels, but the Greeks still managed to destroy half of the Persian fleet.

FACT FILE

Broken pieces of pottery were used for letter-writing in the Greek world. Clay fragments are still found today.

13

WHERE DID THE GREAT RELIGIONS OF THE WORLD BEGIN?

Four-armed Vishnu

The great religions of the world all began in Asia. Three of them – Judaism, Christianity and Islam – began in the same area of west Asia. Hinduism and Buddhism began in India. People all over the world formed systems of beliefs in powers greater than their own. The earliest religions were connected with the forces of nature – the Sun, the Moon, wind, water, rocks and trees – and with animals.

Hinduism is the oldest of the Asian beliefs. There are many Hindu gods and rules governing foods, conduct, festivals and even the jobs which people do. Hindu sculptures of gods and goddesses are full of energy. The four-armed Vishnu is the preserver of the Universe. He is one of Hinduism's two main gods – the other is Shiva.

Buddhism began in India in about 500 BCE, and was later spread by missionaries to Burma and China. In its birthplace of India, Buddhism has practically died out.

FACT FILE

Hindu pilgrims went to bathe in the waters of the holy River Ganges. This tradition is still carried on to this day.

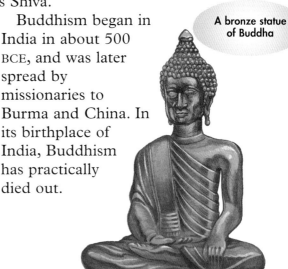

A bronze statue of Buddha

WHERE DOES THE NAME 'DRUID' COME FROM?

The name 'Druid' is derived from 'oak'. *Dru-wid* combines the word roots 'oak' and 'knowledge'. It was Pliny the Elder in his *Naturalis Historia* (XVI 95), who associated the Druids with mistletoe and oak groves:

> 'The Druids . . . hold nothing more sacred than the mistletoe and the tree on which it grows provided it is an oak. They choose the oak to form groves, and they do not perform any religious rites without its foliage . . .'

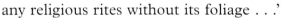

Celtic priests, also known as Druids, have often been identified as wizards and soothsayers. They performed mysterious rites in sacred groves of trees. The Moon, the oak and mistletoe were all magical to the Druids, and so too were many animals. However, in pre-Christian Celtic society they formed an intellectual class comprising philosophers, judges, educators, historians, doctors, seers, astronomers and astrologers. The earliest surviving classical references to Druids date from the 2nd century BCE.

FACT FILE

Around the campfire at night, Celtic poets, storytellers and musicians would pass on tales of the gods and of events in the history of the Celtic people.

WHERE WAS ETRURIA?

Etruria was an area of Italy, known today as Tuscany, Umbria and Latium. Etruria extended from the Arno River in the north to the Tiber River in the south, and from the Apennine Mountains in the east to the Tyrrhenian Sea in the west. It is believed that the Etruscans migrated to Etruria in about 800 BCE from the east, probably travelling by sea. In Etruria, the Etruscans made near-slaves of the people who lived there. The Etruscans then spread north across the Apennines into the Po Valley and south across the Tiber River into Latium and Campania. The civilization reached its height in the 7th and 6th centuries BCE, but in about 510 BCE the Etruscan kings were driven out of Rome, which then became a republic.

FACT FILE

Part of a carved stone relief depicting a Roman funeral procession. The pallbearers carried the dead person on a raised bier, followed by the mourners.

WHERE WERE THE FIRST GLADIATOR GAMES HELD?

The first gladiator games were held in a Roman cattle market in 264 BCE at the funeral of an aristocrat. At the Colosseum in Rome, wild beasts fought in the morning, and the gladiators fought in the afternoon. These cruel battles were justified as hardening Roman citizens to the sight of human bloodshed, so they could endure war better.

A gladiator was a trained warrior who fought bloody battles to entertain the ancient Romans. Gladiators fought using many different types of weapons – a shield and sword, a net and a long three-pronged spear, for example. They usually fought until one of them was killed, but the life of the loser could be spared if the spectators waved handkerchiefs.

WHERE DID THE ROMANS BATHE?

Only wealthy Romans could afford to own private baths, but the city had many public ones. During the time of the emperors, the public baths became luxurious meeting places. They looked like large square or rectangular swimming pools, and were surrounded by gardens, columned marble alcoves and libraries. The bath buildings had facilities for warm and cold baths, steam baths and massages.

The most splendid remains of baths in Rome are those of Caracalla and Diocletian. The Baths of Caracalla date from the 3rd century and are especially impressive; they were decorated with precious marbles, statues and mosaics. The Baths of Diocletian, completed early in the 4th century, were the largest of all the Roman baths and could serve 3,000 people at a time. Most of the site has been built over, but some rooms can still be seen.

FACT FILE

A Roman villa was a large comfortable country home, with hot-air central heating and a courtyard for fine weather. The family had servants to run the house and slaves to work on the land.

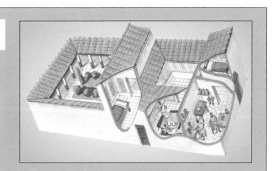

WHERE DID CHARIOT RACES TAKE PLACE?

A hippodrome was the place for horse and chariot races. The ancient Greeks built hippodromes with seats in rows, or tiers. The seats surrounded a long race course, and curved around one end of it.

A wall in the middle divided the course, and it was usually from 180 to 240 m (600 to 800 feet) long. The largest Greek hippodrome was in Constantinople (now Istanbul). The Roman Circus Maximus, like all Roman circuses, was a copy of the Greek hippodromes. The Circus Maximus was the largest of the ancient Roman hippodromes, and seated around 250,000 spectators.

The races were fast and furious, with frequent violent crashes, with winning drivers becoming rich superstars. In more recent times, race tracks, indoor circuses, and amusement places have been called hippodromes.

WHERE WAS THE SILK ROAD?

The Silk Road was a group of ancient trade routes that connected China and Europe. The Silk Road flourished primarily from 100 BCE to AD 1500. The routes stretched across about 8,050 km (5,000 miles) of mountains and deserts in central Asia and the Middle East between eastern China and the Mediterranean Sea.

The Silk Road got its name from the vast amount of Chinese silk carried along it. The cities along the Silk Road provided food, water and rest, as well as goods for trade. Of these cities, Khotan (now Hotan, China) was famous for its jade. The region of Fergana in present-day Uzbekistan was known for its powerful horses.

Camel caravans carried most goods across the dry, harsh regions along the Silk Road. By AD 800, traffic began to decrease as traders started to travel by safer sea routes. A final period of heavy use occurred during the 13th and 14th centuries, when the Mongols ruled Central Asia and China.

FACT FILE

The Chinese were the first to learn to make silk, and they guarded their secret. China was the only supplier of silk until the 6th century AD, when Western countries discovered how to make the fabric.

Where did the Mongols live?

A Mongol *yurt*

Originally the Mongols lived as nomads on the high, grassy steppes of Mongolia and Manchuria (now in China) and Siberia (now in Russia). Their tribes formed a loose group who would come to each other's aid if threatened by outsiders, but in peaceful times would travel with their herds of cattle, goats, camels and sheep from pasture to pasture, carrying their circular, felt homes, called *yurts*, around with them, in much the same way as Mongolian herdsmen do today.

In the late 12th century, the tribes began to unite under a leader, Gengis Khan, and in just over 50 years, he and his successors had conquered lands as far apart as modern-day China, western Russia, and Iran, helped by their fast horses, excellent organisation, and superior military skills, against which their enemies did not stand a chance.

FACT FILE

Mongol warriors were known as superb horsemen and skilled archers, and these abilities helped them to control their vast empire.

WHERE WAS THE BATTLE OF CRÉCY?

The Battle of Crécy was the first major battle of the Hundred Years' War (1337–1453) and fought at the site of the present village of Crécy, in France. The Hundred Years' War began in 1337 and continued for more than a century. It was not a single war, but rather a series of skirmishes between England and France. At Crécy English troops under Edward III defeated a much larger French army under Philip VI. Almost half of the French force was killed in the Battle of Crécy, including more than a thousand knights. English archers on foot proved more effective than the armour-clad French knights on horses. The hero of the battle was Edward, the Black Prince, son of Edward III of England.

FACT FILE

Knights decorated their shield or standard with the heraldic symbols of their own coat of arms. This made it easier to identify the knight in full armour. Each coat of arms had its own unique design.

WHERE ARE THE FORBIDDEN AND IMPERIAL CITIES?

FACT FILE

The first Ming emperor, Chu Yuan-Chang, turned Beijing into one of the greatest cities in the world, with the Forbidden City at its core.

The Forbidden City and the Imperial City lie within the Inner City, an area in Beijing, the capital of China. The Forbidden City includes palaces of former Chinese emperors. It was so named because only the emperor's household was allowed to enter it.

The buildings in this part of Beijing are now preserved as museums. The Imperial City surrounds the Forbidden City. It includes lakes, parks and the residences of China's Communist leaders. The Gate of Heavenly Peace stands at the southern edge of the Imperial City, overlooking Tiananmen Square.

WHERE DOES THE WORD 'FEUDAL' COME FROM?

FACT FILE

A highly ornate gold drinking goblet. Only a very wealthy person could afford costly items like this. Poorer people drank out of leather tankards or earthenware cups.

Feudalism is the general term used to describe the political and military system of western Europe during the Middle Ages. The word *feudal* comes from a Latin term for *fief*. The fief was the estate or land granted by a lord in return for a subject's loyalty and service. Some fiefs were large enough to support one knight; others were great provinces of a kingdom, such as the province of Normandy in France. The church, which owned large fiefs, was also part of the feudal system. Feudalism began to appear in the 8th century. By the 12th century, it had spread from France into England, Spain and other parts of the Christian world.

WHERE WAS THE FIRST TRUE PRINTING PRESS BUILT?

TELL ME WHERE : HISTORY AND EVENTS

FACT FILE

Another early invention was Galileo's telescope, which was more powerful than any that had been used before.

Throughout history, books have been rare and precious things, kept in libraries of monasteries or wealthy houses. Each one had to be copied out by hand with pen and ink, so very few people had the chance to learn to read. The Chinese developed a simple system of printing in the 11th century, but it was only in about 1450 that a German named Johannes Gutenberg built the first true printing press. Using movable metal type, Gutenberg was able to make exact copies of books very cheaply. The first books he printed were the Bible and other religious works. Soon other printers started, and by 1500 they were producing many different sorts of literature, including poems and stories. For the first time, books were available to everyone.

WHERE DID THE PILGRIM FATHERS FIRST LAND?

FACT FILE

In the colonies, girls would embroider samplers – squares of cloth decorated with words and patterns of needlework. They usually added their name and age, as well as the date.

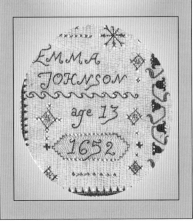

The Pilgrim Fathers were the early English settlers of New England. Originally they were called the Old Comers, then the Forefathers and were not known as the Pilgrim Fathers until the 19th century. The first group of pilgrims set sail from England in 1620 on a ship called the *Mayflower*; they landed in December at what is now Plymouth, Massachusetts in the USA, where they established Plymouth Colony along Cape Cod Bay. Only half of their party survived the first winter. In the following summer a feast was held between the settlers and the local Native Americans in thanks for their survival; it was the first Thanksgiving celebration.

WHERE DID THE PIONEERS COME FROM?

The story of the pioneers tells of the lives of thousands of ordinary people who pushed the frontier of the United States westward from the Appalachian Mountains to the Pacific Ocean. The pioneers headed west to make a better life for themselves and their children. They wanted to improve their social and economic position, while some hoped to have more say in political affairs. Even for those who had money to buy land, good farmland was hard to find in the eastern USA. Across the Appalachians, however, settlers could obtain a plot of fertile land for a fraction of the cost. They

travelled in wagons known as 'prairie schooners' because their white canvas tops looked rather like sails. Settlers moved along the trail in groups for both companionship and safety, and there could be anything up to 100 wagons in a single wagon train.

TELL ME WHERE : HISTORY AND EVENTS

WHERE WAS VOLTAIRE IMPRISONED?

Voltaire was a French philosopher and writer with a keen sense of justice. In the 17th and 18th centuries, a period called the Age of Reason, many people began to regard freedom of speech as a natural right. Such philosophers as John Locke of England and Voltaire of France believed in the importance of the individual. Every person, they declared, had a right to speak freely and to have a voice in the government. Because of these beliefs and for criticizing the government, Voltaire was imprisoned for eleven months in the notorious Bastille prison. The Bastille was a great fortress in Paris that stood as a symbol of royal tyranny.

Voltaire wrote more than fifty plays as well as philosophical stories and poems.

FACT FILE

Voltaire was often a guest at Frederick II's court from 1750 to 1753. Frederick II was the third King of Prussia, and became known as Frederick the Great.

WHERE WAS BONNIE PRINCE CHARLIE'S REBELLION?

Charles Edward Stuart (1720 to 1788) was also known as Bonnie Prince Charlie. He was the grandson of James II, and the last member of the Stuart family to try and claim the throne of England. In the late summer of 1745, Charles landed in Scotland. Many supporters joined his rebellion, especially among the Scottish clans in the north. Within weeks, he occupied Edinburgh. By early December he had marched as far south as Derby in England. But Charles found little support in England and retreated to Scotland. On April 16, 1746, his army suffered a devastating defeat at Culloden Moor, near Inverness. Charles then hid as a fugitive in the Scottish Highlands, until he sailed back to France in September.

FACT FILE

Bonnie Prince Charlie did lead his army to victory over the English in 1745. He was born in Rome and spent the latter years of his life in Italy. His full name was Charles Edward Louis Philip Casimir Stuart.

WHERE WAS GENERAL JAMES WOLFE KILLED?

FACT FILE

By the year 1740 the number of British colonists in North America was approaching one million. Furs and other valuable goods from the colonies, such as tobacco, timber and grain, were sold throughout Europe.

James Wolfe (1727 to 1759) was the British general whose success in the Battle of Quebec in 1759 won Canada for the British Empire. His victory against the French came after several discouraging failures, due in part to his poor judgement.

Before the attack on Quebec, Wolfe moved his troops up the St Lawrence River to a landing well above the city. The troops moved down the river during the night of September 12–13 to a point much nearer Quebec. The Battle of Quebec lasted less than fifteen minutes. Wolfe was wounded twice, but he continued in command until a third bullet struck his lungs. He died just as the French troops were breaking. His greatness as a general has sometimes been exaggerated because of his dramatic death at the moment of victory.

WHERE DID WILLIAM BUILD NORMAN CASTLES?

Conwy castle

FACT FILE

The Bayeux Tapestry was made by the Normans to celebrate their victory over the English in 1066. It is a huge series of pictures depicting incidents during the Conquest.

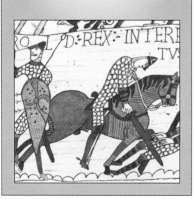

The introduction of castles to England followed the Norman Conquest of 1066. In fact, castles were the means by which William the Conqueror and his followers secured their hold on England following their victory at the Battle of Hastings. William ordered castles to be built at Warwick, Nottingham, York, Lincoln, Cambridge and Huntingdon. These defensive structures helped to secure his newly acquired lands. The first Norman castles were hurriedly constructed of earth and timber.

Conwy castle, in north Wales, is typical of the castles built by the Normans to withstand a long siege. Windsor Castle, Berkshire, is perhaps England's most famous castle.

31

WHERE IS THE SMALLEST INDEPENDENT COUNTRY IN THE WORLD?

The smallest independent country in the world, Vatican City, often just called 'The Vatican' lies entirely within the city of Rome in Italy, west of the River Tiber, and covers only 44 hectares (109 acres). It became independent from Italy in 1929 and has a population of 1,000. It is home to the Pope and the Vatican Offices, which are the civil service of the Roman Catholic Church. The museums in some of the city's buildings house some of the most important works of art in the world. The city has its own radio station and astronomical observatory. It adopted the Euro in 2000.

FACT FILE

St Peter's Basilica is one of the largest Christian churches in the world. The Basilica's giant dome was designed by Michelangelo. It is built on the site of the martyrdom of St Peter, and almost every pope is buried in the crypt.

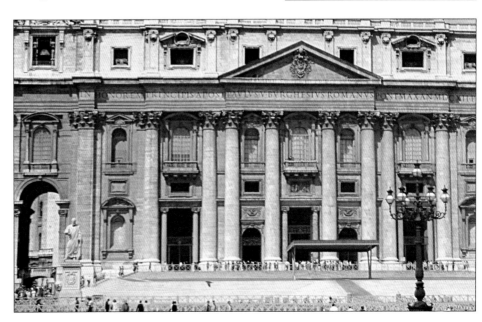

WHERE DID THE CRUSADES TAKE PLACE?

Crusades were the military expeditions organized mainly to recapture Palestine during the Middle Ages. Palestine, also called the Holy Land, was important to Christians because it was the region where Jesus Christ had lived. Palestine lay along the eastern coast of the Mediterranean Sea and Muslims had taken control of it from the Christians. The crusaders, who came from Western Europe, organized eight major expeditions between 1096 and 1270. This was a period when Western Europe was expanding its economy and increasing its military forces. Kings, nobles and thousands of knights, peasants and townspeople took part in the Crusades. They had two main goals: first to gain permanent control of the Holy Land and second to protect the Byzantine empire.

FACT FILE

The word crusade comes from the Latin word *crux*, meaning cross. 'To take up the cross' meant to become a crusader.

33

WHERE DID ALL THE NATIVE AMERICAN TRIBES GO?

Native Americans were the first people to live in the Americas. Their tribes had occupied the land for thousands of years before the Europeans arrived. Each tribe had a distinct and proud culture.

FACT FILE

Many Native Americans died from measles, smallpox and other new diseases introduced by the whites.

As the Europeans moved westward across North America, they were an increasing threat to the Native American way of life. The Europeans 'won' the lands due to their superior weaponry and the remaining tribes were moved onto reservations. Native American culture is deeply connected to the ancestral lands and many of the reservations could not provide the game on which they relied for food. Even today, many Native Americans remain 'outside' US society.

WHERE DID THE UNION PACIFIC RAILROAD RUN?

After the Civil War, the American government encouraged people to settle in the largely empty land of the Great Plains. The Native Americans had already been driven out. The distances involved were enormous and the railways were the key to opening up the huge plains of the mid-western United States of America, providing access for settlers and for trade. The number of locomotives and railroads multiplied rapidly in the United States after 1830. By the year 1869 the Union Pacific Railroad, which linked the east and west coasts of the United States, was finally completed.

A network of other lines spread out across the plains. The railway provided an essential link between remote farming communities and cities, making it easier for people to buy goods and trade their produce.

FACT FILE

The V-shaped metal part on the front of this train is called a 'cowcatcher'. It was designed to push obstacles – including cows – off the line before the wheels hit them.

WHERE DID THE 'SALT MARCH' TAKE PLACE?

Mohandas Gandhi (1869 to 1948), known as Mahatma Gandhi, was one of the foremost spiritual and political leaders of the 1900s. He helped free India from British control by a unique method of non-violent resistance and is remembered by the people of India as the father of their nation. In 1930 Gandhi led hundreds of followers on a 386-km (240-mile) march across India to the sea, where they made salt from saltwater. This was a protest against the Salt Acts, which made it a crime to possess salt not bought from the government. Because of his fight for India's freedom, Gandhi spent seven years in prison. He believed that it was chivalrous to go to jail for a good cause.

FACT FILE

In the middle of the Indian flag is an ancient symbol of a wheel. It is known as the Dharma Chakra, which means the 'Wheel of Law'. India gained her independence from Britain on August 15, 1947.

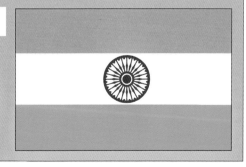

WHERE WAS THE BATTLE OF DIEN BIEN PHU?

Vietnam is a tropical country in southeast Asia. China governed the area from about 100 BCE until 900 AD, when the Vietnamese established an independent state. Fighting broke out between French forces and the Vietminh in 1946. It ended in 1954, with the French defeat at the Battle of Dien Bien Phu. An international conference to arrange a peace settlement also took place at this time. In 1957, Vietminh members in the south of Vietnam began to rebel against the South Vietnamese government. Fighting broke out and it developed into the Vietnam War. The United States became the chief ally of the South.

THE NATURAL
WORLD

CONTENTS

WHERE DOES THE KING PENGUIN PROTECT ITS EGGS?

A king penguin

King penguins do not build nests, but tuck their single egg under their bellies while resting it on their feet, protected by a large fold of skin. Mother and father penguin take turns keeping the egg warm in the cold.

Because the king penguin's main concern seems to be maintaining a constant body temperature, they are limited to places that do not have temperature fluctuations. Their territories can be rocky, icy or snowy, as long as there is water and an abundance of food available. Colonies can be as large as 10,000 penguins, and each bird keeps its distance from the others. In these confined spaces, coming too close earns a nasty jab or flipper slap! The king penguin, second in size only to the huge emperor penguin, is one of the biggest birds, up to 0.914 m (3 feet). They can swim at speeds of 6 mph, and use their wings as flippers to fly through the water, and then hop out onto the rocky shore. Unlike many other penguins, the king penguin runs and doesn't hop while on land.

FACT FILE

Baby chicks are born from their greenish-white eggs nearly naked, but quickly grow a brown woolly fuzz to keep them warm. The adult penguins are often dwarfed by their chicks.

WHERE ARE ELEPHANTS FOUND?

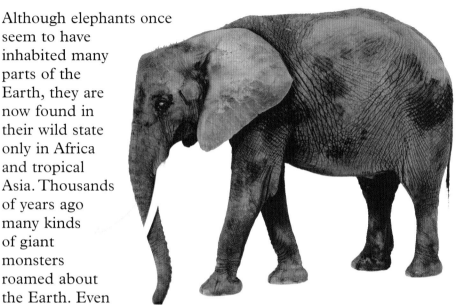

Although elephants once seem to have inhabited many parts of the Earth, they are now found in their wild state only in Africa and tropical Asia. Thousands of years ago many kinds of giant monsters roamed about the Earth. Even though these beasts were immense in size, they were not able to endure the hardships they had to undergo, brought about by climate change and the disappearance of food. One by one they perished until there were only two species remaining, the African and Asiatic elephants.

Elephants are the largest land animals, and in many ways, among the most interesting. They are mild and gentle, reasonably intelligent and easier to train than most other animals.

The most remarkable part of the elephant's body is its trunk. It is an extension of the nose and upper lip and serves the elephant as hand, arm, nose and lips, all in one. There are 40,000 muscles in the trunk.

FACT FILE

The mammoths were ancient relatives of elephants. Their skeletons can be seen in museums. Their bones have been discovered in caves and river beds in North America and Europe.

WHERE WOULD YOU FIND A COBRA?

Cobras can be found throughout the Philippines, southern Asia and Africa, and are well known for their intimidating conduct and deadly bite. Cobras are recognized by the hoods that they flare when angry or disturbed; the hoods are created by the elongated ribs that extend the loose skin of the neck behind the cobras' heads.

The king cobra is the world's longest venomous snake. It averages 3.7 m (12 ft) in length but has been known to grow to 5.5 m (18 ft) and has an olive or brown skin, with bronze eyes. The king cobra is found in the Philippines, Malaysia, southern China, Myanmar (formerly known as Burma), India, Thailand and the Malay Peninsula.

The venom of cobras often contains a powerful neurotoxin that acts on the nervous system. Venoms have some medicinal uses – for example, some are used as painkillers in cases of arthritis or cancer.

FACT FILE

The Spotted Salamander is one of the larger members of the mole salamander family reaching lengths of nearly 20 cm (8 inches) or more. They lay up to 200 eggs in a single mass in early spring to late winter, usually after the first warm rain.

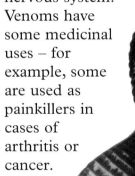

A cobra

WHERE DO RHINOCEROSES LIVE?

There are five different types of rhinoceros living today, of which two – the black rhinoceros and the white rhinoceros – are found in Africa. Both have two horns. The other three kinds live in Asia. The Indian and Javan rhinoceroses only have one horn, while the Sumatran rhino has two horns.

Rhinoceroses have huge, heavy bodies and usually move about very slowly. They pay little attention to their surroundings and do not hunt other animals for food. Rhinoceroses eat only grass and other plants. The great body of the rhinoceros rests on four short legs. Each foot has three toes. Rhinoceroses are hoofed animals and are related to horses.

FACT FILE

This huge creature is normally very quiet and unassuming. But if it is cornered, it can become very fierce and dangerous. A rhinoceros can charge at a speed of up to thirty miles an hour.

43

WHERE DO DOGS COME FROM?

A Jack Russell

All the living members of the dog family are descended from a wolf-like creature called *tomarctus*. This ancient canine, called 'the father of dogs', roamed the Earth's forests perhaps 15,000,000 years ago.

The characteristics and habits of the wild dogs are all shared by the domestic dog. Domestic dogs are brothers under the skin to wolves, coyotes and jackals – the typical wild dogs. All belong to the branch of the dog family called *Canis*. A long time ago early man tamed a few wild dogs. These dogs may have been wolf cubs, jackals or some other member of the wild dog family. People found that these animals could be useful. They used them to help catch other animals and birds for food and clothing.

FACT FILE

As people became more civilized they found that the dog was a good friend and a helpful guard for home and cattle. Over the years breeders have developed about 400 different dog breeds.

Bull Terrier

WHERE WOULD YOU SEE A PUFFIN?

You are likely to see puffins only in early summer on high cliff-tops in remote coastal areas and islands of the British Isles and on the Atlantic coast of Norway, Sweden and Finland. Hugh colonies of puffins nest in burrows in early summer and each pair raises a single chick. During the breeding season both male and female develop the large, brightly coloured beak. In winter they stay far out at sea. Rises in sea temperature because of global warming and overfishing by people have reduced the stocks of sand eels, so their numbers are dropping.

FACT FILE

Although puffins are ungainly while on the grounds and their short wings mean that they are not very agile fliers, they are supremely adapted for swimming underwater, where they catch a kind of fish called a sand eel.

WHERE WOULD YOU SEE A WILD BOAR?

Wild boar used to be common in forests and dense woodland across much of Europe but most of them have been hunted. However, they can still be seen in some areas of southern France and northern Italy, as well as the forests of Eastern Europe. They are also kept for hunting on some large estates. They were accidentally reintroduced into southern Britain when some escaped from a boar farm when a bad storm damaged their pens.

They feed at night and sleep during the day. Despite their large size (an adult male can weigh up to 180 kg (400 lb), they are usually shy animals and avoid human contact if they can. However, if they are cornered or, especially, if their young are threatened, they can be ferocious.

FACT FILE

No other hoofed animal in Europe makes a nest. Although the nest is simple, it does serve to protect the striped piglets for the first few days of life. They gradually lose their stripes as they mature.

WHERE WOULD YOU SEE WILD CATS?

FACT FILE

Wild cats have been known to interbreed with domestic cats, especially when the wild cat lives near human habitation.

Wild cats have been forced, through hunting, to live in remote mountain forest areas. They can be found today in parts of southern and central Europe, with a slowly recovering population in Scotland. They make their dens under fallen trees, amongst rocks or in vacated burrows. Wild cats are about twice the size of a domestic cat, and they also have a thicker, blunt-ended tail. They are shy, nocturnal animals and stay alone except during courtship in early spring. Their diet consists of mainly small mammals, hares, rabbits, birds and amphibians.

47

WHERE WOULD YOU SEE A SWORDFISH?

A swordfish

Swordfish live in tropical and temperate seas, where they feed on fish and, sometimes, squid. They get their name from the elongated upper jaw, on which they spike their prey before juggling it into their mouth and swallowing it whole. They use their speed to catch up with their prey and so need to be able to move very fast through the water, and they have been recorded swimming in short bursts of up to 97 kph (60 mph). Like some other fish, such as sharks, they have no scales to reduce drag. Like some sharks, too, the females hatch their eggs within their body rather than laying eggs, which means that the young are larger before they have to face any predators.

In places like Florida, swordfish are a popular sportfish: because they are so large and so strong, it can take a long time to tire them out so that they can be landed so fishermen regard them as a real challenge.

FACT FILE

A piranha is a sharp-toothed fish that lives in lakes and rivers throughout most of South America. Piranhas have been described as vicious, bloodthirsty predators that can tear a human being to shreds in seconds. In reality, piranhas rarely attack people.

WHERE DID THE FIRST HORSE COME FROM?

Horses evolved over millions of years from far smaller animals in North America. During an ice age, when the sea level was lower than it is now, they spread west to Asia across the land bridge connecting Alaska and Siberia. From there, they spread as far as Europe, Arabia and Africa, evolving into different variations and even species, such as Zebras, to suit their different environments, such as the Tarpan of eastern and southern Europe, the diminutive Shetland pony and the Arab horses, which are renowned for their stamina and speed.

Humans have exploited horses for thousands of years and have selectively bred them to bring out particular characteristics. For example, all race horses in the world are descended from Arab horses. The only truly wild species of horse alive today is the Przewalski's horse from Mongolia.

FACT FILE

A zebra is a striped member of the horse family. There are three species – the common zebra, Grevy's zebra, and the mountain zebra. They live in herds in the deserts and grasslands of eastern and southern Africa.

An Arab horse

WHERE DID SUGAR ORIGINATE?

Sugar cane

Sugars are substances that plants use to store energy, and are known as simple carbohydrates, because they can be broken down in the human body quickly. Several plants store sugars that can be extracted in a form that humans can eat. The first people to extract sugar from sugar cane were South Pacific islanders, who had discovered the process *c*.6000 BC. Sugar cane grows in warm, wet parts of the world, but in cooler climates sugar beet is grown instead. In Canada, sugar is extracted from maple trees in the form of maple syrup. In the 19th century, thousands of slaves were forced to work on plantations in order to satisfy the demand for sugar in America and Europe.

FACT FILE

Several different types of sugar are made by plants. The sugar found in most fruits is called fructose, which is particularly sweet. The sugar in milk is called lactose, while that extracted from sugar cane is known as sucrose. Artificial sweeteners are made to mimic the taste of natural sugars but supply little or no energy.

WHERE DOES STARCH COME FROM?

Like sugar, starch is a substance that plants store for energy. In its most familar forms, such as in wheat, corn, potatoes, beans and rice, it is manufactured by the plants in order to provide energy for the next generation – the seeds – until they can develop roots and small leaves and start making their own. Over thousands of years, man has selectively bred crops that produce larger grains, with more energy in them.

In general, eating wholegrain starchy foods is better for us than

than those that have been heavily processed. For example, brown rice is better than white because white rice has had more of its vitamins and fibre removed during processing so it is easier for the body to break the starch down into sugar quickly. Similarly, brown bread is in general more healthy for us than white.

FACT FILE

Starches are complex carbohydrates that the body takes longer to break down and absorb than sugars and they provide energy for several hours. This is why it is important to have foods like a wholegrain cereal or wholemeal toast for breakfast.

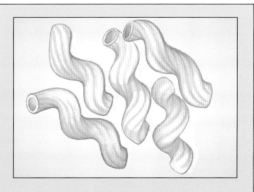

WHERE DOES PEPPER COME FROM?

Pepper is obtained from the seeds (also known as pepper corns) of a climbing shrub – *Piper nigrum* – that grows in Indonesia and India, among other places. The unripe seeds are green, and as they ripen, they turn a pale red. Just before they are fully ripe, they are picked from the bushes and left to dry in the sunlight. Once their skins have gone black, dry and wrinkled, they are ready for collection.

To get black pepper, the pepper corns are simply ground whole, but in order to obtain white pepper, the black skins must be removed before the corns are ground. White pepper has a slightly less strong flavour than black. Immature green peppercorns can be pickled in brine or vinegar and are used widely in cookery, especially in Oriental dishes. Pink peppercorns come from Brazil and are actually from a different species and not true peppers.

FACT FILE

Various aromatic spices come from different plants or trees. *Nutmeg* is a tropical tree that is grown commercially for the spice it provides. *Ginger* is a tangy spice which comes from the underground stem of the ginger plant. *Cinnamon* is the dried bark of a tree. *Clove* is the name given to the dried flower buds of a small, evergreen tree, *Eugenia Aromatica*.

WHERE WOULD YOU FIND FUNGI?

Fungi can be found in all types of habitats and even casual searching in a garden or local park will reveal a variety of species. Most fungi are specially adapted to live in one particular habitat or another. Many species are associated with trees or grow on wood, so woodlands are generally the best hunting grounds. Fungi are organisms that lack chlorophyll, the green matter that many plants use to make food. Fungi cannot make their own food so they absorb food from their surroundings. It is also worth noting that many fungi are seasonal in appearance, fruiting only at certain times of the year. All fungi require moisture to grow and develop, and a dry year can severely affect the numbers of fleshy fungi. Some fungi are so small that you have to look really closely to see them. Examine fallen tree trunks and branches carefully, and look amongst rotting stems and leaves.

FACT FILE

This fungus is popularly called the fly agaric. This is because in medieval times it was used as a fly killer. The fungus was often ground up and added to milk or sugar, which was then set out to attract flies and other insects.

WHERE DO BEES GO IN WINTER?

What happens to the bees in a colony depends on the kind of bee and where in the world they live. For bumblebees, which live in small colonies, only the young queens born in the summer will survive the winter, in a burrow in sandy ground or an abandoned mouse hole. In a honeybee colony, many of the bees will die, but many will live on, feeding on the honey that they have stored during the summer. The exceptions are the drones, who will be driven from the hive as the weather gets cooler because they are not needed during the winter. It is vital that the temperature in the hive does not drop too low, so during the autumn the workers will draughtproof it with a hard amber-coloured substance called propylis and in winter they will use muscle spasms to raise their body heat and thus keep the temperature of the hive at at least 7.2°C (45°F). On warm winter days (when the temperature is above 12°C (53.6°F), they may fly, hunting for nectar from the few flowers that are out, and will clear out rubbish from the floor of the hive.

Red-tailed bumblebee

White-tailed bumblebee

FACT FILE

A typical honey bee colony is made up of one queen, tens of thousands of workers, and a few hundred drones. The queen is the female honey bee which lays eggs. The workers are the sterile female offspring of the queen. The drones are the male offspring.

WHERE DOES SILK COME FROM?

Thousands of years ago China had learned the secret of making silk cloth from the fine web spun by the silkworm, when it makes its cocoon. This secret was jealously guarded, and anyone who carried silkworms or their eggs out of China was punished by death. Today silkworms are raised in China, Japan, India, France, Spain and Italy. The best silk is produced by the caterpillar of a small white moth which feeds on the leaves of the white mulberry. In the early summer each female moth lays around 500 eggs. After the eggs have hatched into tiny black worms, they start to move their heads slowly back and forth. This means they are ready to spin their cocoons. The cocoon, which may contain as much as 457 to 1,097 metres (500 to 1,200 yards) of thread, is finished in about 72 hours.

FACT FILE

The chief substance of most cocoons is silk. But the larva often incorporates other substances, including soil, sand grains, plant materials and hair or waste from its own body.

WHERE DOES A CRICKET PRODUCE ITS SONG?

Crickets are well known for their songs. These songs are produced primarily by the males. Each kind of cricket has a different song, usually trills or a series of chirps. Crickets produce sound by rubbing their two front wings together. They hear sound with organs in their front legs. Their songs help male and female crickets find each other. Male tree crickets sing in chorus. Their song is a high-pitched treet-treet-treet.

Cricket

A cricket is a type of jumping insect related to the grasshopper. Crickets differ from grasshoppers in several ways. The wings of most crickets lie flat over each other on top of their backs. Other crickets only have tiny wings or are wingless. The slender antennae are much longer than the body in most kinds of crickets.

Crickets are commonly found in pastures, meadows and along roads. Sometimes they even enter houses. These insects eat plants and the remains of other insects. The best-known are the house cricket of Europe and the common cricket of the United States.

Grasshopper

FACT FILE

A grasshopper is an insect that can leap about 20 times as far as the length of its body. If a human being had that same leaping ability, he or she could jump about 37 m (120 feet).

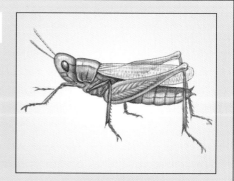

WHERE IS A CLAM'S FOOT?

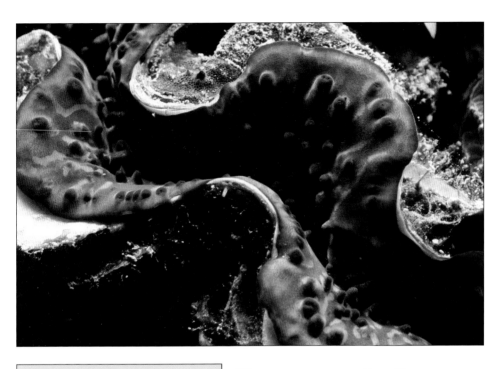

FACT FILE

The giant clam lives on coral reefs in the Red Sea, the Indian Ocean and the western Pacific. These clams can grow to a length of more than 1.2 m (4 feet).

Clams are a type of mollusc, a group of soft-bodied animals that have no bones. They use a large, muscular organ called a *foot* to burrow in mud or sand. The foot spreads beneath the body, and its muscles move in a rippling motion that makes the animal move forward. A clam is an animal whose soft body is covered with a protective shell. They also have a heart, blood vessels and kidneys. Clams live on the bottom or along the shores of oceans, lakes and streams in many parts of the world. They feed on tiny water organisms called plankton, or on small, shrimp-like animals.

57

WHERE WOULD YOU FIND A FIG FLOWER?

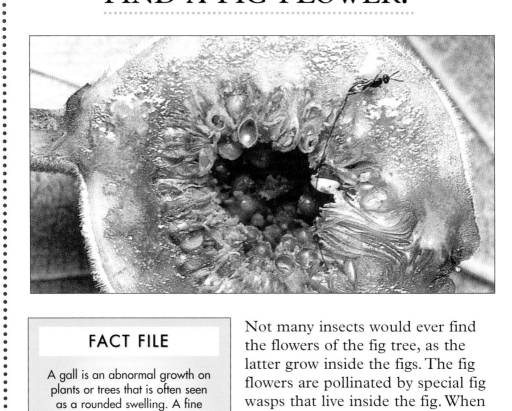

FACT FILE

A gall is an abnormal growth on plants or trees that is often seen as a rounded swelling. A fine example is an oak apple pictured below. Galls are caused by parasites that feed and live on the plant.

Not many insects would ever find the flowers of the fig tree, as the latter grow inside the figs. The fig flowers are pollinated by special fig wasps that live inside the fig. When the flowers are producing pollen, some wasps leave. They move into another fig, carrying pollen with them on their bodies and so fertilize that one.

Figs have been cultivated for thousands of years, and are mentioned in Arabian, Egyptian, Greek and Roman texts. When ripe they are very soft and so must be transported very carefully. They can also be dried to provide a good way of sweetening foods in winter when there is little other fruit around.

WHERE DID THE NAME BUTTERCUP COME FROM?

Buttercups (*Rananunculus acris*) get their name from their bright buttery yellow colour and the cup shape that the young flowers have. They flower in early to mid-summer and are common in wildflower meadows, pastures and roadside verges. They grow to about 30 cm (12 in) in height. Other wildflowers in the same family include creeping, hairy and bulbous buttercups, lesser celandines and water crowfoot. An old child's game was to hold a buttercup under your chin: if the yellow colour was reflected on your skin, you liked butter!

FACT FILE

Strangely, cows do not eat buttercups because of their acrid taste, so farmers look on them as weeds. They can quickly take over an area because they spread so rapidly and grow faster than other flowers so they get the lion's share of the light.

WHERE DID THE SPRINGBOK GET ITS NAME?

FACT FILE

Red deer are fascinating creatures to watch during the autumn rut. This is when the stags drive off rivals with roaring challenges, clashes of antlers and dramatic fights to secure a 'harem' of hinds.

The springbok is small antelope that lives on the *veldt* (grassy plains) of southern Africa. *Bok* is the Afrikaans word for buck, and these pretty little animals are also called springbucks. Their main predators are lions and cheetahs, and if the springbok spot one of them, they distract the predator and warn the other members of the herd by leaping up to 2 m (6½ feet), more than double their own height, into the air, displaying the white flashes on their rumps, before dashing off. There used to be large herds of springbok in southern and southwestern Africa, but many were killed by huntsmen and farmers. They are members of the cattle family.

WHERE WOULD A COCKATOO BE A PEST?

Cockatoo

Cockatoos are large members of the parrot family that are native to Australia and New Guinea. There are several species, which may be a mix of white, grey, black, rose-pink or red, but the best known is the sulphur-crested cockatoo. Like all cockatoos, they have a large crest on their heads that they can raise and lower. They are strong birds and use their beaks to help them to climb.

In fruit- and nut-growing areas of Australia they can pose problems for farmers because they feed in large

Macaw

flocks and can ruin a vast area of an orchard in just minutes.

They are clever birds, and can be trained to talk, although their usual call is a loud, raucous screech, which can be heard ringing through eucalypt forests and public parks and gardens across much of eastern and northern Australia.

FACT FILE

Many species of parrots are prized for their ability to repeat words or to learn complicated tricks. The famous pirate Long John Silver, from the story *Treasure Island*, was renowned for having a parrot on his shoulder.

WHERE DO FROGS LAY THEIR EGGS?

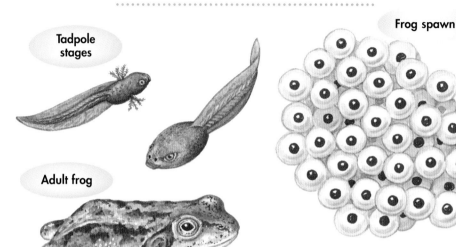

Tadpole stages

Frog spawn

Adult frog

Frogs are amphibians and so they have to go back to water to breed. The females lay their eggs (frogspawn) in water, attached to a plant, and these then absorb water and swell up. Depending on the species of frog and the temperature, the eggs can take up to a few weeks to hatch and will slowly turn from tadpoles to small frogs. During this change (called *metamorphosis*), they will lose their gills and develop lungs and their tail will be absorbed into their body as they develop legs.

The way to tell the difference between frogspawn and toadspawn is that frogspawn is in clumps while toadspawn is laid in strands.

FACT FILE

In northern countries, when cold weather sets in, some frogs dive into a pond, bury themselves in the mud and stay there all winter. Ponds do not freeze solid, even when winters are very cold, so the frog does not freeze either.

A wolf

WHERE IS A WOLF'S TERRITORY?

Wolves are among the largest members of the dog family and they live in communal groups called packs. Each pack has a territory, which they will not allow other wolves to enter. The size of the territory depends on how much prey is available: if food is scarce, a territory will be large whereas if prey are plentiful, a territory can be small.

Packs are tightly knit groups, led by an alpha male and an alpha female, who are dominant over the other members. Often, only the alpha female will breed, in order to avoid there being too many cubs to feed.

Wolves are among the best cooperative hunters in the animal kingdom and their howls allow them to keep track of which member of the pack is where during a hunt. They typically hunt large mammals, such as deer, elk and caribou.

WHERE WOULD YOU SEE A CONTOUR FEATHER?

Jay

A feather is one of the light, thin growths that cover a bird's body. Birds can have two main kinds of feather – contour and down. The parts of a feather vary, depending on its type. Contour feathers grow on a bird's body only in special areas called pterylae. From the pterylae, the relatively large contour feathers fan out to cover the bird almost completely. Down feathers, however, are found on all parts of a bird's body. Feathers consist chiefly of keratin, a substance also found in the hair of mammals and the scales of fish and reptiles. Unlike hair and scales, feathers have a complicated branching pattern. Feathers enable a bird to fly and help it maintain a constant body temperature. Although feathers are remarkably durable, they gradually wear out. Birds shed their feathers and grow a new set at least once a year. This process is called moulting.

FACT FILE

People have used feathers for a variety of purposes. For hundreds of years American Indians used feathers to make arrows and head-dresses. Until the mid-19th century, when pens with steel nibs became popular, most people wrote with quill pens. Today, manufacturers use feathers as stuffing in pillows and upholstery.

WHERE IN THE WORLD WOULD YOU FIND THE MOST PIGS?

There are about 860 million pigs on farms throughout the world. China has the most, over 40 per cent of the world total. About one-fifth of the farms in the United States raise pigs – about a quarter of the meat eaten in the United States comes from pigs.

There are many different kinds of pigs reared around the world. As pigs have a short reproductive cycle, new breeds can be developed over a relatively short period of time. Pigs reproduce rapidly and can mate when only about eight months old. Sows carry their young for about 114 days before giving birth, usually to 8 to 12 piglets at a time. Pigs reach maturity at $1\frac{1}{2}$ to 2 years of age and can live from 9 to 15 years.

FACT FILE

A pig has four toes on each foot. Each toe ends in a hoof. The two middle hoofs are divided on all pigs, except the Mule-foot breed. Mule-foot pigs have a solid, or single-toed, hoof in the middle of each foot.

WHERE WOULD YOU FIND A KOLA NUT?

Kola nut

Kola nuts are the seeds from the fruit of 125 species of tree from the tropical rainforests of west Africa, which are now also widely cultivated in South America, the Caribbean and Asia. The nuts are either white or red and are irregularly shaped. They contain caffeine and theobromine, which are mild stimulants and the extract from the nuts is used in soft drinks such as colas and in medicines such as pain killers and cold remedies.

In western Africa, they are often used as ceremonial gifts and in the past were chewed both for their mildly stimulant effect and because they could remove hunger pangs.

FACT FILE

Most nuts are rich in protein and fat, though chestnuts and a few others have more starch than protein. In Italy, bread is sometimes baked with a flour made from chestnuts.

WHERE DOES A COCONUT GROW?

Coconuts originally grew only in Southeast Asia and Melanesia, but now they are grown across all areas of the world that are warm enough. They often grow next to the coast of tropical islands as they have been carried there by the ocean currents.

A coconut

Coconuts grow in clusters among the feathery fronds at the top of coconut trees. The large green husk and rind surround the hard, brown shell, inside which are the white coconut meat and the thin liquid called coconut milk.

In coconut plantations, the nuts are harvested several times a year, but will fall naturally after about a year when they are ripe. Products that are made from the flesh include copra, desiccated coconut, creamed coconut and coconut milk. The husk is used to make ropes, mats and plant compost.

FACT FILE

The peanut plant is unusual because its pods develop underground. For this reason peanuts are often called groundnuts. Peanuts are a nutritious food. There are more energy-giving calories in roasted peanuts than in the equivalent weight of steak.

WHERE WAS THYME FIRST USED?

Today, thyme is used as a kitchen herb, but originally the dried leaves were burned in temples in ancient Greece to create an incense in religious ceremonies. The plants are native to the Mediterranean region and there are about 300–400 species, a few of which are used in cooking, including common thyme and lemon thyme.

Common thyme has hairy stems and paired elliptical leaves and its flowers are usually lilac and form in circles round the stems. It is a member of the mint family and is popular in many savoury dishes.

The essential oil in thyme is used in aromatherapy as an antiseptic and the extract thymol is used in a number of simple medicines such as cough mixture.

FACT FILE

Rosemary is an evergreen shrub of the mint family noted for the fragrance of its leaves. Rosemary is used fresh or dried as a herb for cooking. The plant also yields an oil used in perfumes.

WHERE WOULD YOU FIND A FOX'S DEN?

FACT FILE

A female fox gives birth to her young in late winter or early spring. A young fox is called a cub. Red foxes have between 4 and 9 cubs in one litter. The male takes no part in bringing up the cubs.

The common type of fox in Europe is the red fox. Contrary to popular thought, foxes are not members of the dog family. In the wild, foxes may dig their own burrow, take over a disused badger sett or nest in a hollow log. Urban foxes may nest under garden sheds or even under the floorboards of old houses. Usually the female (vixen) will only move to a den a short while before she is due to give birth.

Once the cubs are big enough to be left, she will find food for herself. After about five weeks she will start to bring small animals, such as rabbits and birds, for her cubs to eat. When they are strong enough, she will bring back live mice, frogs, rats or small birds so the cubs can practise hunting techniques.

69

WHERE ARE AN OWL'S HORNS?

Owls have short, thick bodies, strong, hooked beaks, and powerful feet with sharp claws called talons. Some owls have tufts of feathers on their heads. The tufts are called 'ears' or 'horns'. Their feathers are long, soft and fluffy and often make the birds appear larger than they really are. Their plumage is usually fairly dull so they can blend in with their surroundings.

An owl is a type of bird that usually lives alone and hunts for food when it is dark. The owl has been called the 'night watchman of our gardens' because it eats nuisance rodents at night. There are about 145 species of owl, and they live throughout the tropical, temperate and subarctic regions of the world. They can also be found on many oceanic islands.

FACT FILE

The eyes of most owls are directed forward. For this reason owls can watch an object with both eyes at the same time. Owls cannot move their eyes in their sockets, they must therefore move their heads to watch a moving object.

WHERE DOES A HEDGEHOG GO IN WINTER?

In winter a hedgehog goes into hibernation, which is a sleeplike state. It hibernates to protect itself against the cold and reduce its need for food. The hedgehog's body temperature becomes lower than normal and its heartbeat and breathing slow down greatly. An animal in this state needs little energy to stay alive and can live off fat stored in its body.

A hedgehog is a small animal that looks somewhat like a porcupine. It has short ears and legs, a short tail and a long nose. Stiff, needlelike growths, called spines, cover its back and protect the animal from its enemies. When it is in danger, the hedgehog rolls itself into a spiny ball.

FACT FILE

A hedgehog may have two litters between May and August. They have about five young which open their eyes at two weeks. They can roll up from 11 days and are weaned by six weeks.

GENERAL KNOWLEDGE

CONTENTS

· · · · · · · · · · · · · · · · · · ·

WHERE DID ICE CREAM ORIGINATE?

The origins of ice cream can be traced back to Rome in the 4th century BCE. The Roman emperor Nero ordered ice to be brought from the mountains and combined it with fruit toppings. In the 13th century, Marco Polo learned the Chinese method of creating ice and milk concoctions and brought it back to Europe. Over time, recipes for ices, sorbets and milk ices evolved and were served in the fashionable Italian and French royal courts.

The use of ice mixed with salt to lower and control the temperature of the mix of ingredients proved a major breakthrough in the creation of ice cream as we know it. The invention of the wooden bucket freezer with rotary paddles facilitated its manufacture. It was a Baltimore company that first produced and marketed ice cream wholesale in 1851. The treat became both distributable and profitable with the introduction of mechanical refrigeration.

FACT FILE

During the 20th century many brands of ice cream were marketed on a large scale in supermarkets. Ice cream sundaes have also become very popular desserts with people of all ages.

WHERE WERE THE FIRST CLOWNS SEEN?

Clowns were first seen in the ancient Egyptian courts around the year 2270 BCE. The comic spirit of clowning exists in just about every known culture. It is as old as civilization and makes us laugh, whatever age we are.

The western tradition of clowning can be traced to ancient Greece where strolling clowns were seen in Sparta as early as the 7th century BCE; they were called *deikeliktas* or 'those who put on plays'. These clowns portrayed everyone from soldiers, fools, and witches to slaves and Greek gods.

Throughout the Middle Ages and early Renaissance, jesters or fools maintained the art of clowning in the palaces of kings and great nobles. Jesters played an important role in the social culture of medieval Europe. They could answer back to kings, bishops and all in authority, by making fun of anyone and satirizing social customs. During this period, jesters adopted a standard uniform of bright green and saffron coats, hose and a hooded cap which was topped by tiny bells designed to tinkle whenever the wearer moved.

TELL ME WHERE : GENERAL KNOWLEDGE

FACT FILE

America's first circus came about when a sea captain, called Hachaliah, returned from China bringing an elephant with him. He had purchased the elephant for $10,000 and named him 'Old Bet'. He managed to teach Old Bet, and other animals, various tricks as a form of entertainment.

WHERE WAS PAPER FIRST MADE?

The first people to use a form of paper for keeping records and correspondence were the ancient Egyptians more than 5,500 years ago. They layered strips of the stems of the papyrus plant (Cyperis papryus), crushed them and hammered them to form a loose-textured writing material. Before this, people in Mesopotamia had used a sharp stylus to make symbols and letters in tablets of clay. Their form of writing is known as cuneiform, while the Egyptian script developed into hieroglyphics.

The first people to make paper by a simplified version of the process that is still used today were the Chinese, who about 2,000 years ago learned to crush hemp and parts of the mulberry tree to a pulp to separate out the fibres, which were then cleaned and made into thin sheets and dried. Later improvements include adding a filler such as china clay to make the surface smooth.

FACT FILE

The first person to develop a process for making paper in rolls rather than sheets was Nicholas Louis Robert, who designed a machine to do this in 1798.

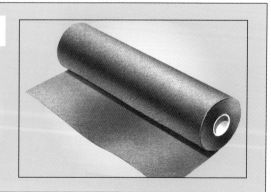

WHERE DID THE CABBAGE COME FROM?

Cauliflower

Savoy cabbage

FACT FILE

Lettuce is a popular vegetable that is similar in many ways to cabbage. It is used chiefly in salads, and people usually eat it fresh and uncooked. Lettuce farming probably began in Persia as early as 550 BC.

Cabbage, Chinese cabbage, broccoli, kale, curly kale, Brussels sprouts, Savoy cabbage, purple sprouting broccoli, red cabbage, white cabbage, spring greens, calabrese and cauliflower are all varities of the same species (*Brassica oleracea*). They are all derived from wild cabbage, which grows on sea cliffs, where its thick, waxy leaves help it to withstand salt blown on the wind. Sea kale grows on the sea shore, but is a different species. As well as these varieties, which have been developed over thousands of years, there are hundreds of cultivated varieties, including ornamental cabbages, which are sold as garden plants and are mostly inedible.

WHERE WOULD YOU SEE A JOEY?

A joey is a common name in Australia for the young of a variety of marsupials. Although the name is particularly associated with kangaroos and wallabies, it also applies to young koalas, wombats and possums. Marsupials are a group of mammals that give birth when their young are very small and then carry them in a pouch on their belly. A young koala will spend the first seven months of its life in its mother's pouch and the following six months clinging to her back before becoming independent.

Koalas eat only eucalyptus leaves and shoots, which are extremely tough and contain little nutrition, so the koalas spend most of the day sleeping wedged in the fork of the tree while their digestion gets to work. They are mainly active for short periods at night, when it is cooler and moving takes less energy. They are becoming endangered in many places because of deforestation, road accidents, forest fires and disease.

FACT FILE

Kangaroos are also marsupials, with their young completing development in a pouch on the belly of the mother. Kangaroos have large, powerful hind legs and small front legs. Large kangaroos can hop as fast as 48 km (30 mi) per hour for short distances.

WHERE IS THE FESTIVAL OF CARNIVAL?

Rio de Janeiro in Brazil has won fame for an annual festival called Carnival. Carnival features four days and nights of parades and dancing in the streets. The festival of Carnival, with its spectacular street parades and vibrant music, has become one of the most potent images of Brazil. Its roots lie in the European Mardi Gras, a lively festival, which precedes the fasting and prayers of the Roman Catholic holy season of Lent. In Brazil it seems to have first occurred in Bahia in the mid-17th century and in Rio de Janeiro in the 1850s, where it was associated with street parades and elegant private balls. Carnival did not take on its present spectacular form in Rio until the 1930s, when the dance known as the samba emerged in the shanty towns of the city.

FACT FILE

One of the most popular celebrations in Japan is the New Year's Festival, which begins on January 1 and ends on January 3. During the festival, the Japanese dress up, visit their friends and relatives, enjoy feasts, and exchange gifts.

WHERE IS THE THAMES BARRIER?

The Thames Barrier is in East London, near Greenwich. It was opened in 1982. It is needed because there is an increased risk of flooding. London is sinking into the clay on which it is built, and because northern Britain is rising as it recovers from the weight of ice that covered it in the last Ice Age, the southeast of Britain is tilting downwards. Thirdly, and most worryingly, climate change is melting the ice caps and leading to a rise in sea levels. If a high tide occurred at the same time as a bad storm, which would also raise sea levels, without the barrier a flood could destroy large parts of London. If predictions about rising sea levels and worse storms caused by global warming are true, the barrier will need to be replaced by a bigger one in a few years.

FACT FILE

Floods can also occur inland, when heavy rain drains off the land and causes rivers to burst their banks. This effect is made worse in built-up areas where the rain cannot soak into the ground.

WHERE DID WRESTLING FIRST TAKE PLACE?

FACT FILE

King Henry VIII was an accomplished sportsman and excelled at hunting and wrestling. Henry also loved music and could play, sing and dance.

Wrestling as an organized and scientific sport was probably introduced into Greece from Egypt or Asia, but there is a Greek legend that it was invented by the hero Theseus. The first recorded wrestling match in Japan took place in 23 BCE. The Japanese have a style of wrestling that is called 'Sumo' in which weight is very important.

Wrestling is one of the earliest sports known to man. Many hundreds of scenes of wrestling matches are carved on the walls of ancient Egyptian tombs. They show nearly all the holds and falls known to us today, so wrestling was a highly developed sport at least 5,000 years ago.

WHERE WAS THE FIRST MAGIC PERFORMED?

The first magic was performed in ancient Egypt. The Egyptian magician Dedi, who lived about 2700 BCE, gave a performance in which he decapitated two birds and an ox and then restored their heads. Other Egyptian magicians were noted for their skill with the trick of the cups and balls. In this trick small balls seem to pass invisibly from one inverted cup or bowl to another. Finally, they are converted into larger spheres or such unexpected items as oranges or live baby rabbits.

One of the greatest box-office attractions in the history of magic was the feat of appearing to saw a woman in half. In the first performance of this act in London in 1921, the British magician Percy Tibbles, whose professional name was P. T. Selbit, cut through a box that contained a woman assistant. She emerged unharmed.

FACT FILE

The word *rune* comes from a Gothic word meaning secret. A rune is any one of the characters of the earliest written alphabet (as seen on this runestone). Runic characters were probably first used by pagan priests in making charms and magic spells.

WHERE DOES THE WORD 'ROBOT' COME FROM?

The word 'robot' comes from '*robota*', the Czech word for drudgery. They are able to perform repetetive tasks, such as spray painting cars, welding metal and assembling machinery. They are controlled by computer programmes. They are particularly useful in places that are too hazardous for humans to work in, such as areas of nuclear power stations or reprocessing plants where radiactivity is very high.

Very few robots looks like the humanoid ones (androids) of science fiction, but Japanese scientists have been developing prototypes for several years.

Perhaps the most exciting use of robots is in exploration, such as the rovers – Spirit and Opportunity – that NASA sent to Mars. Future rovers will have such advanced computer-processing power that they will be able to select between different options using their own software, rather than having to wait for instructions from scientists on Earth.

FACT FILE

Robots are used to test special clothing such as spacesuits and firefighting clothes, to ensure that they are safe for humans to wear.

WHERE WOULD YOU HAVE SEEN SMOKE SIGNALS?

The best known smoke signals were used by Native Americans to send simple coded signals to each other over long distances. Different information could be given by varying the amount of smoke in each puff and the length of time between the puffs. These could be about the whereabouts of enemies or perhaps the presence of game.

Smoke signals were, however, developed much earlier as a means of communication between the towers along the length of the Great Wall of China. In both systems, the code has to be understood by both the sender and the receiver. The ancient Romans used fire in a similar way on places such as Hadrian's Wall. The Roman system had the advantage that it could be used at night.

Semaphore, which was invented in France in the 1790s, used a series of towers with two black poles that could be positioned at four angles to represent particular letters, words or symbols. They devised a code that consisted of nearly 8,500 words and phrases. A more efficient version using shutters was developed in Sweden at the same time, but both were superseded by Samuel Morse's invention, the electric telegraph.

FACT FILE

Only a few hundred years ago the fastest way a piece of news could travel was to be carried by a person on horseback. Today, however, we can talk instantly to people all over the world via communication satellites.

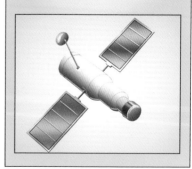

WHERE WAS THE FIRST COWBOY HAT MADE?

Whilst on a hunting trip in the Wild West, the son of a Philadelphia hat maker created the first cowboy hat in 1865. His name was John B. Stetson. As the story goes, John B. Stetson and some companions went west to seek the benefits of a drier climate. During a hunting trip, Stetson amused his friends by showing them how he could make cloth out of fur without weaving. Stetson used the fur from hides collected on the hunting trip. Kneading the fur and working it with his hands, dipping it into boiling water, spreading it out, kneading it, and dipping it again, he created a soft, smooth piece of felt. Stetson made an unusually large hat out of this fur-felt. He then wore the hat for the remainder of his hunting trip, at first as a joke, and then later he grew fond of the hat for its protection from the weather.

FACT FILE

A milestone was achieved in 1814 by a French magician named Louis Comte; he became the first conjurer on record to pull a white rabbit out of a top hat.

WHERE WOULD YOU SEE CUPID?

In Roman mythology, Cupid was the god of love, the son of Venus, the goddess of love and Mars, the god of war. In modern culture, he is the symbol of romantic love and is most often to be seen nowadays on Valentine cards. He is usually drawn as a chubby, blond, curly-haired, playful figure, with tiny wings, and armed with a bow and a quiver of arrows, which he aims at men and women to make them fall in love. In Greek culture, he was Eros, and his statue can be seen in London's famous Piccadilly Circus. In both Greek and Roman mythology his story is the same. Venus was jealous of the beauty of the human princess Psyche and ordered Cupid to make her fall in love with the most monstrous being imaginable. Cupid accidentally scratched himself with his arrow tip and fell deeply in love with Psyche. He forbade her to ever look at him and when she disobeyed he left in anger. Psyche searched the world for him and was rewarded by Jupiter for her constancy. He made Psyche a goddess, so that she and Cupid could marry and live happily ever after. Today, Cupid is the most popular symbol of everlasting love. 'Love' is frequently depicted as a heart pierced by two of Cupid's arrows.

FACT FILE

England's greatest poet and playwright, William Shakespeare (1564–1616) wrote many plays about love, one of the most famous being *Romeo and Juliet*.

WHERE DO BANANAS GROW?

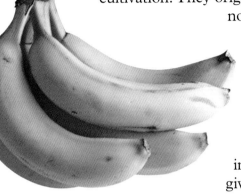

There are some 100 species of banana in cultivation. They originated in Asia, but are now also grown in Africa, India, northern South America, the Canary Islands, Australia and the Caribbean. They like hot, wet climates, but some species can also be grown under glass in cooler regions if they are given sufficient water and are heated during the winter.

Banana plants can grow to 9 metres (30 feet) high. Despite their size, they are not trees. After flowering, the stems die back. The flower spikes emerge from the top of the plant's stem and curve over. The male flower is at the end of the spike and the female flowers are part-way along its length.

Bananas are a very healthy food because they contain carbohydrates to give you energy, fibre, the minerals potassium and phosphorus and vitamins A and C.

FACT FILE

A cluster of bananas is called a hand and consists of 10 to 20 bananas, which are known as fingers. At least five hands of bananas grow on the stem of each banana plant. During World War II, it was nearly impossible to get bananas in Britain.

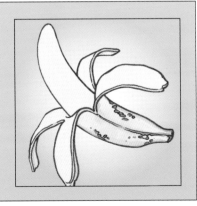

WHERE DID THE IDEA OF A GLIDER COME FROM?

During the late 18th century, people made the first flights in the air using balloons, which were an early form of airship. After the first balloon flights, inventors tried to develop a heavier-than-air flying machine. Some inventors experimented with gliders or engineless planes. They studied birds' wings and discovered that the wings were curved. By building gliders with curved wings instead of flat ones, they could make the vehicles fly hundreds of feet. But long-distance flight in a heavier-than-air machine did not become possible until the invention of an engine light enough but powerful enough to keep a plane in flight. The first such engines were four-stroke gasoline engines, developed during the 1880s and initially used to power bicycles, boats and carriages.

FACT FILE

In 1903, the brothers Orville and Wilbur Wright – two American bicycle makers – made the first successful powered airplane flights in history near Kitty Hawk, North Carolina.

WHERE DO WE INHERIT OUR TRAITS?

Living things inherit characteristics, often called traits, from their parents through heredity. Heredity is the passing on of biological characteristics from one generation to the next. The process of heredity occurs among all living things – animals, plants and even such microscopic organisms as bacteria. Heredity explains why a human mother always has a human baby and why a mother dog has puppies and not kittens. It is also the reason offspring look like their parents. You resemble your parents because you inherited your hair, nose shape and other traits from them. All organisms consist of cells. Tiny biochemical structures inside each cell called genes carry traits from one generation to the next.

FACT FILE

You may look like your parents, but you are not an exact duplicate of either of them. You inherited half your genes from your father and half from your mother.

WHERE WOULD YOU FIND A WELL?

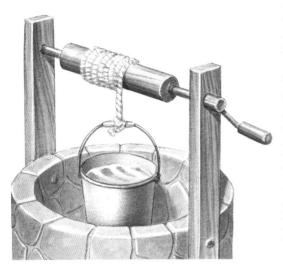

In some areas of the world there is no piped and purified water supply, either because it is too remote an area or, because it is too expensive. Here, people rely on wells for drinking water. The simplest well is just a hole in the ground, lined with bricks or stone, sunk deep enough to reach the natural level of the under-lying water - the water table. Water is drawn up by hand or pumped to the surface.

An artesian well is sunk deeper into a layer of porous water-bearing rock (an aquifer) that lies between two layers of rock that water cannot pass through (impermeable rock). If the well is sunk into the low-lying layer of porous rock, natural water pressure will force the water up the well shaft. If the pressure is insufficient, it will need to be pumped or hauled up. Springs occur naturally where the end of an aquifer reaches the ground's surface. Spring water is usually free from pollutants, and often contains minerals from the rock through which it has travelled. We call this mineral water.

FACT FILE

Niagara Falls is one of the most spectacular natural wonders of North America. The energy of the crashing water at the falls has been used since 1891 to generate electricity.

WHERE WOULD YOU FIND A SHERPA?

You would find the Sherpa people in Nepal high up in the Himalayas. They are renowned for their mountain climbing abilities. Many Sherpas earn money by guiding tourists, trekkers and mountaineers up the steep and rocky paths. The Sherpas originally migrated to Tibet from Mongolia and then left Tibet to settle in the Solo Khumbu district of Nepal. Tenzing Norgay (1914–1986), a Sherpa guide, became one of the first two people to reach the top of Mount Everest and return. On May 29, 1953, Tenzing and Sir Edmund Hillary of New Zealand reached the 8,850-m (29,035-foot) summit. Their expedition had spent more than two months moving supplies and equipment up the mountain. Tenzing had tried six times previously to reach the top of Everest. He grew up in Thamey, a village in the Solo Khumbu, a district inhabited by Sherpa people in Nepal near the base of Mount Everest. After his ascent with Hillary, Tenzing became internationally famous and a hero to the Sherpa and Nepalese people.

FACT FILE

Mountains and hills cover most of Japan, making it a country of great beauty. Many Japanese people keep fit by mountain climbing.

WHERE DOES THE ALPHABET START WITH QWERTY?

The alphabet starts with QWERTY on a typewriter, computer keyboard or 3G mobile phone or notebook. The first practical typewriter was invented by Christopher Latham Sholes, and was marketed by the Remington Arms company in 1873. The action of the type bars in early typewriters was very sluggish, and tended to jam frequently. To solve this problem, Sholes obtained a list of the most common letters used in English and changed his keyboard from an alphabetic arrangement to one in which the most common pairs of letters were spread fairly widely apart on the keyboard. Because typists at that time used what was known as the 'hunt-and-peck' method, Sholes's arrangement increased the time it took for the typists to hit the keys for common two-letter combinations – long enough to ensure that each type bar had time to fall back sufficiently far to be back in place before the next one came up.

FACT FILE

Most computer keyboards resemble typewriter keyboards in the arrangement of their letter keys, but have additional keys for special computer functions.

WHERE WOULD YOU FIND A FAX MACHINE?

In the 21st century, you might find a fax machine in a legal department where identical duplicates of papers and correspondence are vital and maybe coming from a source that is not able to scan the original onto a desktop computer printer/scanner. The fax machine was a revolutionary introduction into the

Fax machine

modern office in the mid-1980s, although Scottish inventor, Alexander Bain was granted a patent for his creation in 1843, and his concept remained the basis for the affordable 20th century fax-machine. A fax machine consisted of an optical scanner for digitizing images on paper, a printer for printing incoming messages and a telephone for making the connection. Fax facilities are now often incorporated into computer and desktop printers and the quality of the images and speed of transmission is incomparably faster than was possible in the 1980s. Handwritten notes, illustrations, photographs, documents and three-dimensional images can now be sent by e-mail, via the Internet, and downloaded in seconds and printed if necessary.

FACT FILE

Before the telegraph, a system called semaphore, in which a sequence of lights or other markers, such as flags, signalled from point to point. However, semaphore systems did not work well at night or in bad weather.

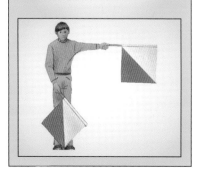

WHERE DID PEOPLE FIRST GROW FLOWERS?

Orchid

Tiger lily

FACT FILE

Primrose is the common name for a group of plants that usually flower in the early spring. Cultivated primroses are considered choice ornamental garden flowers. Many of these have been developed from the common primrose, which grows naturally in the woods and meadows of Europe.

Flowers grow in most places on the Earth's surface, except where it is too hot, dry or cold. Scientists have found fossils of flowers from many millions of years ago, when dinosaurs roamed the planet. When humans became farmers several thousand years ago, they would have grazed their animals on wild plants, including flowers, but gradually learned to cultivate the best plants and to use them for food and in herbal medicine, and eventually they grew the prettiest ones for their flowers alone.

The people of ancient Mesopotamia (now Iraq) had beautiful gardens, and we know from ancient Egyptian royal tombs that they had gardens in which they cultivated flowers and several pharaohs' mummies were discovered with garlands of flowers.

WHERE DID AGRICULTURE BEGIN?

Agriculture was developed in different regions of the world at different times. People in southwest Asia began to grow cereal grasses and other plants about 9000 BCE. They also domesticated goats and sheep at about that time, and later they tamed cattle. In southeastern Asia, people had begun to cultivate rice by about 7000 BCE. People who lived in what is now Mexico probably learned to grow food crops about 7000 BCE. The invention of farming paved the way for the development of civilization. As prehistoric people became better farmers, they began to produce enough food to support larger villages. In time, some farming villages developed into the first cities.

FACT FILE

Aquaculture is the controlled raising of aquatic animals and plants, of which seaweeds account for about 25 per cent. Aquaculture is an ancient occupation. Chinese people practised aquaculture between 3,500 and 4,000 years ago.

WHERE WOULD YOU FIND A PERISCOPE?

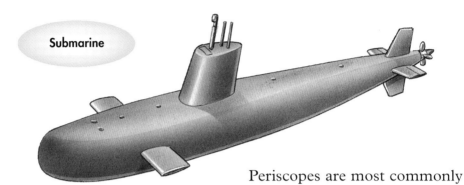

Submarine

Periscopes are most commonly associated with submarines, but they can also be used by tanks, military helicopters and individuals. The simplest version is a tube with one opening at the top front and another at the bottom rear. Inside are two mirrors, set at 45° to the tube and parallel to each other. An image of what the top opening of the periscope is pointed at is reflected from the top mirror down to the bottom mirror and then out of the lower opening so that the viewer can see it. In a battle, this allows the viewer to see over the top of walls or trees so he can shoot at the opposition without exposing himself to their fire. This simple sort of periscope was used in the trenches in northern Europe in World War I.

Submarine periscopes are more complicated as they have prisms instead of mirrors and lenses that magnify the image. Tank and helicopter periscopes can both be rotated through 360°. Some modern submarines use electronic imaging techniques instead of mechanical periscopes.

FACT FILE

The armed forces also use helicopters to observe the movements of enemy troops and ships. Many naval helicopters have devices to locate and track submarines.

WHERE DO ALMONDS COME FROM?

Almonds are nuts that originally come from southwest Asia, and they also grow wild in many eastern Mediterranean countries. They are now grown commercially in many countries around the Mediterranean, including Spain, Greece, Italy, Syria, the Lebanon, Portugal, Morocco and Turkey, as well as Iran, Australia, California and India. They are also grown farther north in Europe but here the climate is less reliable.

The brown-skinned edible kernel is surrounded by a grey leathery hull, which hardens and splits when the fruit is ripe. There are two types of almonds: sweet almonds generally have white flowers and bitter almonds usually have pink flowers.

Ground sweet almonds are the basis for marzipan and can be used as a flour-substitute in low-carbohydrate diets, and in almond butter, which is a substitute for peanut butter. Almond oil is extracted from sweet almonds and is commonly used as a massage oil. In food, it is used as a flavouring substitute for olive oil. Bitter almonds contain the poison prussic acid.

FACT FILE

Walnut growers once left walnut shells that fell to the ground as waste. Today, the shells are collected and used in glues and plastics. They are also used to make solutions for cleaning and polishing metal surfaces.

WHERE DID TRAMPOLINING START?

It has been said trampolining started in Alaska where the Eskimos used to toss each other up into the air on a walrus skin. This was done in a similar way to the sheet used by firemen to catch people jumping out of the windows of houses which are on fire. In Anchorage airport, Alaska, there are postcards showing Eskimos being tossed into the air from a walrus skin.

FACT FILE

In the early 1930s, George Nissen made a trampoline in his garage and used it to help with his diving and tumbling activities. He then felt that he could entertain audiences and also let them participate in his demonstrations.

There is also some evidence of people in England being tossed up into the air by a number of people holding a blanket. These may or may not be the true origins of the sport of trampolining but it is certain that in the early years of the 20th century there were stage acts which used a 'bouncing bed' on the stage to amuse audiences. The bouncing bed was in reality a form of small trampoline covered by bedclothes on which the acrobats performed mostly comedy routines.

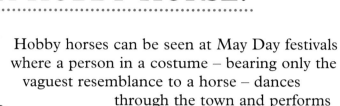

WHERE WOULD YOU SEE A HOBBY HORSE?

Hobby horses can be seen at May Day festivals where a person in a costume – bearing only the vaguest resemblance to a horse – dances through the town and performs various rituals. This festival is related to other nature-based British folk customs such as Morris dancing. At one time many towns all over England had hobby horses, but few are left today. The best known is at Padstow, in Cornwall, where it was spelled and pronounced as 'obby oss', and some may have wondered at the appearance of this strange creature, and its even stranger antics! There is a well-known nursery rhyme about the hobby horse of Banbury, in Oxfordshire:

Ride a cock horse to Banbury Cross,
To see a fine lady ride upon a white horse,
Rings on her fingers and bells on her toes,
She shall have music wherever she goes.

A child's toy was made as a result of the festival horse, which consisted of a horse's head on the end of a long stick.

FACT FILE

For centuries, the role of the belly dance in Middle Eastern society has been that of a folk dance that people would perform at joyous occasions such as weddings, the birth of a child or community festivals.

WHERE WERE THE FIRST VIOLINS MADE?

The violin was first made in Italy during the 16th century. It is a four-stringed instrument that is rested under the chin while a bow made of horsehair is drawn across the strings. This causes the strings to vibrate, providing a great flexibility in range and tone.

Early stringed instruments were played by plucking the strings with the fingers. The origin of stringed instruments played by rubbing the strings is linked to the appearance of the bow. The very first bow was a simple stick before the hair-bow was adopted.

Exquisitely crafted instruments created by the Italian master Antonio Stradivari continue to be the most highly prized musical instruments in the world. His design for the violin has served as a role model for violin makers for more than 250 years. Stradivari also made harps, guitars, violas and cellos – more than 1,100 instruments in total. About 650 of these instruments survive today.

Not only can the violin be played as a solo instrument, it is also the predominant instrument of the orchestra. A symphony orchestra uses more than thirty violinists.

FACT FILE

The history of bongo drumming can be traced to the Cuban music styles known as Changüi and Son. These styles first developed in eastern Cuba in the 19th century about the time that slavery was abolished.

WHERE WOULD YOU HAVE CAUGHT THE PONY EXPRESS?

You would have caught the Pony Express between Saint Joseph, Missouri and Sacramento, California. It was a horseback mail service which began on 3 April, 1860. At that time, regular mail delivery took up to three weeks to cross America.

The Pony Express carried mail rapidly overland on horseback nearly 2,000 miles between St. Joseph and Sacramento; the schedule allowed ten days for the trip. The mail was then carried by boat to San Francisco. Each rider was expected to cover 120 km (75 miles) a day. Pony Express riders were usually lightweight young men, often teenagers, who used special saddle bags that could be moved to a fresh horse very quickly at a change station. The Pony Express route was extremely hazardous, but only one mail delivery was ever lost. The regular Pony Express service was discontinued in October 1861.

FACT FILE

A pigeon post was in operation while Paris was besieged during the Franco-Prussian War of 1870 to 1871. People used the pigeons to carry messages in and out of Paris.

WHERE WERE JIGSAW PUZZLES FIRST MADE?

Jigsaw puzzles were first made in the 1760s when European mapmakers pasted maps onto wood and cut them into small pieces. The 'dissected map' became a very successful educational tool and has been used in many schools to help children with their geography. The 18th century inventors of jigsaw puzzles would be amazed to see the transformations of the last 250 years. Children's puzzles have changed from educational toys to entertainment, showing different subjects such as animals, nursery rhymes and modern tales of super heroes and Disney characters. But the biggest surprise for the early puzzle makers would be how adults have taken to puzzles over the last century. Puzzles for adults started about 1901 and by 1908 they had become a full-blown craze. Nowadays they are made of printed paper on cardboard. Jigsaws can also be completed for free on the Internet, with a choice of infinite cuts and numbers of pieces.

FACT FILE

The first known published crossword puzzle was created by a journalist named Arthur Wynne from Liverpool, and he is usually credited as the inventor of the popular word game.
It appeared in a Sunday newspaper, the *New York World*, on 21 December, 1913.

¹P	I	²T		³O
E		⁴R	⁵A	N
⁶G	⁷A	O	L	
	⁸C	U	P	S
⁹P	E	T		

WHERE DID ART NOUVEAU GET ITS NAME?

Art Nouveau refers to the 'new' art that was produced during the two decades preceding and following the start of the 20th century. Sigfried Bing, a dynamic German-born Parisian and patron of the arts, is credited with providing the name for this movement. In 1900, he opened a shop called *L'Art Nouveau Bing*, that eventually became identified with the international decorative arts movement which it supported. Nowhere was the style of Art Nouveau more pronounced than in France, and no name more recognizable than that of René Lalique. Trained as a jeweller, René Lalique opened his *atelier* in Paris in 1895. His avant-garde designs were highly sought after and his most famous client was Sarah Bernhardt, the tragic actress who exemplified the Art Nouveau woman. Heralded as the finest and most innovative jewellery designer at the 1900 *Exposition Universelle* in Paris, Lalique never stopped experimenting and learning. In 1907, he began to work in an entirely different art form – designing glass perfume bottles. In 1912, at the age of 50, Lalique opened his first glass factory and began to produce perfume bottles, tableware, vases, lamps and all types of objects for a lady's boudoir.

FACT FILE

The ancient Greeks believed that diamonds were splinters of stars fallen to the earth. It was even said by some that they were the tears of the gods.

WHERE CAN CANDLES BE TRACED BACK TO?

FACT FILE

Candle clocks were used in the 9th century but were not very accurate as a draught could cause the candle to burn more quickly.

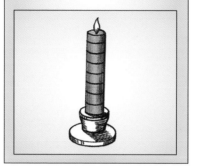

Candles can be traced back as far as biblical times. For many years they were the main source of light for peoples' homes. Many early Greek and Roman candles were made of flax thread coated with wax and pitch, while in other countries candles were made of palm oil, coconut oil, beeswax and olive oil. In England bayberry wax was refined for use in making candles. The earliest dipped candles were made of tallow. It was not until the 19th century that paraffin replaced tallow as the main ingredient for candlemaking.

WHERE WAS THE FIRST NEWSPAPER PRINTED?

The first printed newspaper appeared in Germany in the late 15th century in the form of a news pamphlet or broadsheet, often highly sensational in content.

The history of newspapers goes back at least five centuries. In Renaissance Europe handwritten newsletters circulated privately among merchants, passing along information about everything from wars and economic conditions to social customs and 'human interest' features.

In the English-speaking world, the earliest predecessors of the newspaper were *corantos*, small news pamphlets produced only when some event worthy of notice occurred. The first successful published title was *The Weekly Newes* of 1622. The first true newspaper in English was the *London Gazette* of 1666.

FACT FILE

The history of printing can be traced back thousands of years, to when people in the Middle East learned to press carved designs into wet clay. Today, publishers can complete every step in the production of books, magazines and newspapers by electronic means.

OUR

WORLD

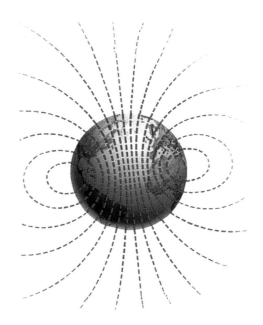

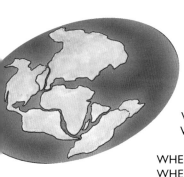

CONTENTS

· · · · · · · · · · · · · · · · · ·

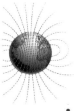

WHERE IS LIBERTY ISLAND?

Liberty Island is in New York Harbor, near Manhattan Island. It is known all over the world because it is the site of the Statue of Liberty, which was designed by Frédéric Auguste Bartholdi and built by Gustav Eiffel in the 1880s as a present from the French people to commemorate the United States' Declaration of Independence a century before. The statue, which is made of plates of copper on a steel frame, is 46 m (151 ft) tall and weighs 204 tons. The statue stands in the remains of Fort Wood, an early 19th-century fort. The area of the fort was declared a national monument in 1924, and the rest of the island was included in the monument in 1937. The Statue of Liberty overlooks Ellis Island, which was the main point of immigration for hundreds of thousands of people from Europe and Africa during the 19th and early 20th centuries. The statue's full title is *Liberty Enlightens the World*, reflecting the long-held American belief that they should be an example and a force for good in the world.

FACT FILE

The people of France gave the Statue of Liberty to the people of the United States in 1884. This gift was an expression of friendship and of the ideal of liberty shared by both countries.

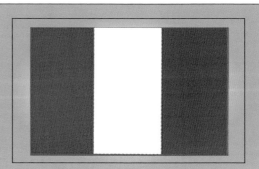

WHERE IS THE SNOW LINE?

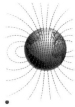

The snow line is the lower limit of the area on a mountain where snow is present all year. It is not at the same height everywhere: in Africa it is far higher than it is in the Alps of Europe or the Rocky Mountains in North America because the surrounding lands are hotter. In any location, it is not even the same from year to year as more snow will melt in hotter summers. In many parts of the world, the snow line is, like glaciers, retreating up the mountains as climate change seems to be causing longer, hotter summers and shorter, winters with less snowfall.

FACT FILE

Artificial snow is produced at some ski resorts. It is made from partly frozen droplets of water. Machines make this 'snow' by spraying a mixture of freezing water into the air.

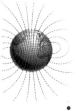

WHERE DOES A HURRICANE BEGIN?

Devastation caused by a hurricane

Hurricanes form in the Atlantic and east Pacific oceans, when the surface temperature of the ocean is at least 27°C (81°F) over a wide, deep area and the conditions in the atmosphere are right. Because they are fuelled by warm water, they lose their strength over land. They are divided into categories, with category 1 the least and category 5 the worst. As well as the high winds, damage is caused by hail, heavy rainfall that can cause mudslides and storm surges, which cause flooding. In 2005, hurricane Katrina's storm surge caused more damage than the winds when it breached the flood defences at New Orleans. Elsewhere such storms are called typhoons and tropical cyclones.

FACT FILE

Approximately 85 hurricanes, typhoons and tropical cyclones occur in a year throughout the world. Hurricanes are most common during the summer and early autumn.

WHERE WOULD YOU FIND BIG BEN?

Big Ben is one of London's most famous landmarks, although correctly, Big Ben is the name of the largest bell in the Clock Tower (sometimes called St Stephen's Tower) of the Palace of Westminster, where the United Kingdom's Houses of Parliament sit.

The Palace of Westminster was rebuilt after a fire in 1834 destroyed almost all of its predecessor. The clock was installed in 1854 and the tower was finished in 1858. When the original 14.5-tonne bell was tested, it broke in half and had to be recast as a 12.5-tonne bell, which, although cracked, is still in use today.

If it were not for all London's traffic noise, the bell could be heard chiming 15 km (9 miles) away.

FACT FILE

Some clocks register time on a 24-hour basis. On such a clock, 9 a.m. would be shown as 0900 and 3 p.m. would be 1500. This system avoids confusion between the morning and evening hours.

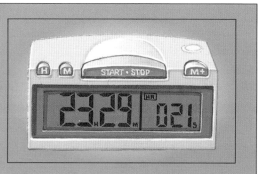

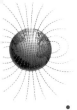

WHERE IS THE ALPINE SLOPE?

The Alpine Slope is part of the Alps, a mountain range in south central Europe. The landscape includes huge mountains and deep valleys with forests of beech, oak, and chestnut trees growing on the lower slopes of the mountains. At higher levels there are grasslands and pine forests. Only low bushes grow at still higher elevations, while the mountaintops are covered in rocks and glaciers. Melting snow from the Alps feeds many rivers. Hydroelectric plants along alpine rivers provide much of Italy's electric power. The people of the alpine region live in small, scattered communities, and make their living by farming and herding. Many tourists visit the Alps to ski.

FACT FILE

The Apennines stretch almost the entire length of Italy. These mountains have steep inclines of soft rock that are constantly being eroded as a result of heavy rains, overgrazing of sheep and goats, and the clearing of forests for timber and farmland.

WHERE ARE THE 7 NATURAL WONDERS OF THE WORLD?

Although there is no official list, the following are generally accepted as the Seven Natural Wonders of the World. In the United States **Meteor Crater**, also known as Barringer Crater, is a huge circular depression in the earth near Winslow, Arizona, caused by a meteorite impact and the **Grand Canyon** is a breathtaking 450-km (280-mile) chasm created by the Colorado River eroding the rock of the Colorado plateau over about 6 million years. Asia's **Mount Everest**, rising 8,850 metres (29,035 feet) above sea level in the Himalayas, is the world's highest mountain. In central Australia **Uluru** (Ayers Rock) rises 346 metres (1,141 feet) above the desert floor and off the east coast the **Great Barrier Reef** is the world's longest coral reef formation at about 2,010 km (1,250 miles) in length. Europe's **Matterhorn**, on the Italian-Swiss border, is one of the most beautiful mountains on Earth and in southern Africa, the spectacular **Victoria Falls** is on the Zambezi between Zimbabwe and Zambia.

FACT FILE

Uluru (Ayers Rock) is loaf-shaped and has a circumference of about 9 km (5¹/₂ miles). It is composed of red sandstone. It is a sacred site for the local Native Australians.

WHERE ARE THE HIMALAYAS?

The Himalayas is a vast mountain range formed by the crumpling of the Earth's surface as India moves northwards and collides with Asia. They form an arc 2,410 km (1,500 miles) long between India, Pakistan and China, with Nepal perched among them. The highest mountains in the world are found in this mountain chain. Of the individual peaks, the best known are Everest and Kanchenjunga, as well as K2 and Nanga Parbat in the Karakoram range, a northwestern extension of the Himalayas. The snows of the Himalayas are vital to people south of the range because they feed great rivers like the Ganges, Indus and Brahmaputra.

FACT FILE

Many animals that live in tropical, temperate and cold regions live in the Himalayas. Tiger, leopard, rhinoceros, elephant, yak and several kinds of monkey can be found there.

WHERE DID THE FIRST FORESTS DEVELOP?

The first forests on Earth developed in the Devonian Period, between 416 and 359 million years ago in swampy ground near the coasts. The first forests were quite low-growing and consisted of ferns and similar plants, but these evolved rapidly and grew quite tall. Fossils of *Archaeopteris* – tree-like ferns that date from the late Devonian – have been found in Europe, Morocco, North America and Australia. They are related to the tree-ferns that are found today in Australia, Malaysia and New Zealand. At the end of the Devonian, trees almost 30 m (100 feet) tall were not uncommon and the first seed-bearing plants had evolved. Such trees form the oldest coal seams on Earth.

FACT FILE

As plants colonized the land during the Devonian Period, animals were not far behind. Marine animals adapted to life on land and scorpions, mites, centipedes, spiders and early amphibians are known to have existed.

Scorpion

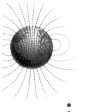

WHERE DO TROPICAL RAIN FORESTS GROW?

Tropical rain forests grow near the equator, in regions where it is hot and wet almost all year round. The biggest areas are in the Amazon Basin of South America and the Congo Basin in West Africa. The rain forests are important because they have a wide diversity of plants and animals. They are also very important in absorbing large amounts of carbon dioxide, one of the major greenhouse gases, and so help to slow down the greenhouse effect, which is why conservationists wish to prevent destruction of the rain forests. The forest canopy at the tree tops is very dense, so not much light reaches the forest floor, except in clearings where old trees have fallen, which are rapidly colonized by small plants.

FACT FILE

The canopies of the rain forests are where most of the animals live. Many, like monkeys, stay in the tree-tops almost all of the time, only coming to the ground in order to move to another tree that is too far away to reach by jumping.

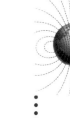

WHERE DO TROPICAL SEASONAL FORESTS GROW?

Tropical seasonal forests grow in the tropics and subtropics in regions where there is a wet season and a dry season, but it is not as hot or wet as areas where rain forests grow, such as India, parts of China, Pacific islands, parts of northern Australia, and central and central-south America. While the trees in the rain forests are evergreen, deciduous and evergreen trees are found in tropical seasonal forests. In addition, more shrubs and small plants can grow, forming what is called the understorey. In China, the understorey often contains bamboos, while in Australia tree ferns can be seen. There is a wide range of animals in these forests, including lizards, birds, monkeys, bats, snakes and a large number of insects.

FACT FILE

Bamboos and palms may form a dense shrub layer, and a thick herb layer blankets the ground. The animal life resembles that of the rain forest, and includes the sloth.

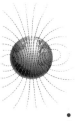

WHERE IS THE GREAT SALT LAKE DESERT?

FACT FILE

Bathers and sailors enjoy using the Great Salt Lake. Swimmers float easily in the salty water. Many visitors go to Antelope Island, which is the lake's largest island, a state park, and home to a herd of wild buffalo.

The Great Salt Lake Desert is west of Salt Lake City in Utah in the western United States. Mineral-rich waters are brought to the lake and then evaporate (there is no outlet to the sea), leaving the minerals behind. Great Salt Lake and other smaller lakes in the area are the remnants of Lake Bonneville, which was far bigger, but also had no outlet to the sea for most of its history. The desert is the salt layers deposited by this lake's evaporation. Like the Dead Sea, the waters in some parts of the lake are saline enough for people to float on, but unlike the Dead Sea, the Great Salt Lake is visited by large colonies of wading birds. The level of the waters in the lake can fluctuate rapidly: at one time the waters were so high that water had to be pumped out, while in recent years, lack of rainfall has caused the lake to shrink.

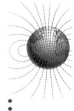

WHERE IS THE WORLD'S LARGEST HOT DESERT?

The world's largest hot desert is the Sahara in northern Africa. It stretches from the Atlantic Ocean in the west to the Red Sea in the east. As well as the sand dunes that people associate with deserts, it also has high, rocky plateaux, mountains and areas of semi-desert. The only water apart from minimal seasonal rainfall is found in oases and in the river Nile. Today, people live around the edge of the desert and some live at or travel between the oases, but thousands of years ago when it was wetter, people also lived in the desert's interior and many of their cave and rock paintings – called petroglyphs – have been found.

Because a desert is defined by the amount of rainfall or snowfall it receives, the largest desert in the world is, in fact, the icy continent of Antarctica.

FACT FILE

An oasis is a fertile patch in a desert which surrounds a water hole. This water comes from underground wells or springs. The Sahara has about 90 large oases, where people live in villages and grow crops.

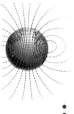

WHERE IS THE WORLD'S FIRST NATIONAL PARK?

FACT FILE

Old Faithful is a relatively predictable geyser, whose eruptions occur between 55 and 102 minutes apart, depending on the size of the previous eruption: bigger eruptions have longer intervals between them. The largest geyser in the park is Steamboat Geyser.

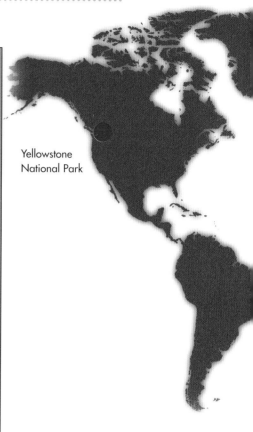

Yellowstone National Park

Yellowstone National Park was established in 1872 and covers parts of Wyoming, Montana and Idaho. It is famous for its geothermal springs and geysers, such as the spectacular Old Faithful. These result from continuing volcanic activity under the area. The whole area is sitting over a series of calderas caused by a supervolcano (the caldera is the crater left after a massive eruption in which the magma chamber is emptied rapidly and the ground above collapses into it). The supervolcano under Yellowstone is the result of a 'hotspot', a plume of molten lava rising from deep within the earth. About 2.2 million years ago, a massive explosion blew 2,500 km^3 (600 mi^3) of material into the air covering most of North America in ash. The park's stunning landscape is home to bison, bears, elk, American bald eagles and trumpeter swans.

WHERE WOULD YOU SEE A BILLABONG?

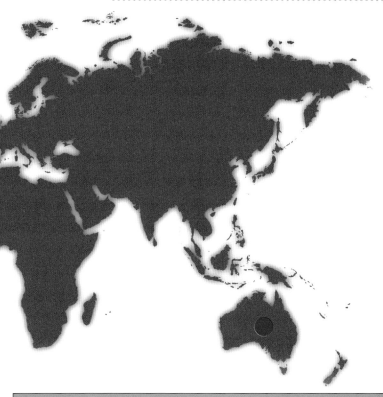

FACT FILE

Australia is the only country that is also a continent. In area, Australia ranks as the sixth largest country and smallest continent.

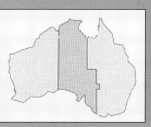

You would find a billabong in the Outback of Australia. The word comes from the local Native Australian term meaning 'dead river'. They are formed when a river or stream changes course or cuts across a bend leaving an oxbow lake that eventually becomes detached. In some places where rainfall is scarce, billabongs only last for a few months, during which time they are popular watering holes for flocks of parrots, kangaroos and feral camels.

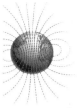

WHERE IS THE MENAI BRIDGE?

The Menai Suspension Bridge spans the Menai Strait between Anglesey and the Welsh mainland. It was built by Thomas Telford from 1819–1826 and spans 176 m (579 ft).

The roadway is suspended by 16 chain cables, made of 935 iron bars each, that carry the weight to the two huge concrete towers. It was by far the longest suspension bridge to be built until that time. Fourteen years later, Robert Stephenson built the Britannia Bridge nearby to carry a new railway line that ran to the port of Holyhead.

The longest suspension bridge in Britain is the Humber Bridge. Completed in 1981, it is 2,200 m (6,770 ft) long, with a central span of 1,410 m (4,700 ft).

FACT FILE

During the Middle Ages, movable bridges called drawbridges were built over the moats of many castles in Europe. Most bridges were made of stone or wood until the late 18th century, when cast iron and wrought iron came into wide use.

Erie Canal

WHERE WAS THE FIRST IMPORTANT US WATERWAY?

Joining the Hudson River to either Lake Erie or Lake Ontario by canal was first suggested in 1699, but work was not started until 1817 and the original canal was completed in 1825. By linking New York with the Great Lakes, the Erie canal opened up areas of the northern United States to settlement and farming. The original canal was 584 km (363 mi) long, 12 m (40 ft) wide and 1.2 m (4 ft) deep and ran from Albany on the Hudson River via Troy (where the Champlain Canal split off) to Buffalo on Lake Erie. Its course, which ran through the Mohawk river valley was chosen because it was the only way through the Appalachian Mountains this far north. The 183-m (600-ft) difference in height was spanned by a total of 83 locks.

FACT FILE

The Erie Canal was originally designed for barges to be drawn by horses or mules, but after it was deepened and widened, it could be used by shallow-bottomed steam barges.

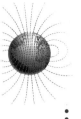

WHERE WAS TOBACCO FIRST SMOKED?

Tobacco plants (*Nicotiana tabacum*) are native to northern South America, and the inhabitants of central and South America had been smoking the dried leaves in pipes long before the Spanish arrived in 1492. Christopher Columbus took some seeds back to Europe with him and the plant was developed as a mild relaxant. Popular ways to take tobacco included in pipes, as snuff and rolled into cigars and hand-rolled cigarettes. Chewing tobacco became popular in America in the nineteenth century. Tobacco is widely grown in areas that are warm enough, and Cuba is particularly well known for the quality of its cigars.

As well as the nicotine that acts as a stimulant and makes tobacco addictive, the leaves contain tar and other chemicals that have been proved to cause lung cancer and to contribute to heart disease and stomach ulcers. Chewing tobacco can cause cancer of the mouth.

N. tabacum is one of more than 60 nicotiana species, and most of the rest are grown for their beautiful flowers.

FACT FILE

Tobacco contains small amounts of nicotine, a substance that acts as a stimulant on the heart and other organs. Nicotine also stimulates the nervous system, causing many people to become addicted to it.

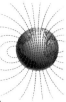

WHERE IS THE ART OF FLORICULTURE PRACTISED?

Floriculture is the industry of growing ornamental plants for sale as plants to grow in pots or flower beds or as cut flowers. Tender plants are grown in glass houses that can be kept warm in winter, while more hardy species and varieties can be grown out of doors.

Growing flowers for cutting is a huge industry in the Netherlands, where there is, in particular, a tradition of growing tulips.

Growers use many sophisticated techniques to ensure that plants and flowers mature at exactly the correct time: making flowers bloom early is called 'forcing', while making them bloom late is called 'holding back'. Such techniques are used to ensure, for example, that daffodils are at their best for Mothering Sunday and roses for St Valentine's Day.

FACT FILE

Flowers can now be flown anywhere in the world within a few days, and floriculture is becoming an important export industry for some African countries such as Kenya.

WHERE WAS THE BIRTHPLACE OF THE RENAISSANCE?

The Renaissance (which is French for rebirth) began in several cities, but its full flowering is seen best in Florence. The term is used to describe the cultural movement from the fourteenth to seventeenth centuries, after the Middle Ages, when ancient Greek and Roman texts, statues and buildings were rediscovered and classical learning was 'reborn'. During the Renaissance, many of the greatest artists – including Michelangelo, Leonardo da Vinci, Donatello, Brunellschi, Giotto and Raphael – worked here.

FACT FILE

Leonardo da Vinci was not just a great artist, but was also a theoretician, military architect anatomist and experimental scientist. He designed, flying machines that look remarkably like modern helicopters, military equipment, submarines and an armoured car.

WHERE IS THE WINTER PALACE?

The Winter Palace is in St Petersburg, in northwestern Russia, near the mouth of the Neva River, on the Gulf of Finland. St Petersburg was the imperial capital of the Russian Empire, and the Tsars and their courtiers built many palaces here. The Winter Palace was designed by Bartolomeo Rastrelli in a Baroque fashion, and was built between 1754 and 1762, during the reign of Empress Elizabeth, but the first royal resident was Catherine the Great. The palace, which suffered a major fire in 1837 but was beautifully rebuilt, now holds part of the collections of the State Hermitage Museum, has 1,057 halls and rooms, 1,786 doors and 1,945 windows. The Hermitage holds art from almost every era of western art, as well as collections of oriental and central Asian art.

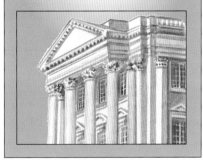

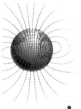

WHERE IS CARACAS?

Caracas is the capital city of Venezuela and lies in the narrow valley of the River Guaire in the north of the country, just inland from the Caribbean Sea, at about 750–900 m (2,500–3,000 feet) above sea-level. It was founded in 1567 by Spanish settlers who were looking for gold. Although many districts were badly damaged by an earthquake in 1812, which the Spanish claimed was divine retribution for the natives rebelling against their rule, there are several areas with old colonial buildings. The historic centre of the city is called Libertador, after Simón Bolívar, the Liberator, who led much of northern South America to revolt against European rule in the early nineteenth century. The central plaza is also named after him.

FACT FILE

Caracas is one of the most highly developed and richest cities of South America because the profits from Venezuela's rich oil industry have been ploughed back into its economy.

WHERE DO THEY SPEAK QUECHUA?

FACT FILE

The highland Amerindians of Peru live at elevations up to 4,570 m (15,000 ft). Almost all highland Amerindians are farmers. Many of the older people still wear traditional garments of handwoven cloth.

Quechua is the language that was spoken by the Incas. Various dialects are still spoken by some 10 million people in Bolivia, Argentina, Brazil, Peru, Ecuador, Colombia and Chile. After the Spanish and Portuguese conquests, these became the official languages, although Quechua has now become a joint official language in both Peru and Bolivia.

Because the Incas had not developed writing, Quechua is still primarily an oral language spoken by people of Amerindian descent, while people of mixed Amerindian-Spanish descent, known as mestizos, and people of pure Spanish descent speak Spanish. A related language that is spoken in parts of Peru is Aymara, and this is spoken in the east of the country.

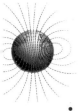

WHERE MIGHT YOU FIND HOUSES ON STILTS?

Houses on stilts are found in several parts of the world, such as South-east Asia, Papua New Guinea, western Africa and the Amazon basin and in the Orinoco valley of South America.

They are commonly found on the shores of rivers and lakes, and were widely used in prehistory. In Europe, both Neolithic and Bronze-Age stilt houses have been found in Austria.

For people who make their living from fishing and for whom it is easier to get from place to place by boat, building homes by the lake shore is sensible and building them on stilts makes it possible to reduce the damage caused by flooding.

In Scotland, crannogs were built from about 3200 BC on. These are dwellings built on stilts in the middle of lochs, or on small islands in them, and reached by a narrow causeway. These could be defended more easily than houses on the loch shore.

TELL ME WHERE : OUR WORLD

WHERE WERE ORANGES FIRST GROWN?

The orange tree (Citrus sinensis) is a hybrid that was developed thousands of years ago in South-east Asia, possibly in southern China, India, Vietnam or Pakistan. It is properly known as the sweet orange to distinguish it from the bitter orange. The name comes from the Persian word, *narangi* or the Sanskrit word *naranga*. It is thought to be a hybrid between a pomelo and a tangerine. There are several different varieties, such as navel, blood, Jaffa and Seville oranges. Many of these were developed in the nineteenth century by cross-breeding other citrus species.

> **FACT FILE**
>
> The skin of the orange fruit is called the zest and the soft, white layer beneath it is the pith. The pith contains pectin, the substance that helps to set jam and marmelade.

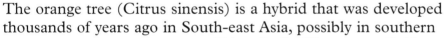

The trees can grow up to 10 m (33 feet in height) and bear flowers in spring. Like some other citrus fruits, such as the lemon (*C. limon*), the fruits may take a year to ripen, and the following year's flowers bloom before the fruits from the previous year are ready to pick.

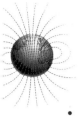

WHERE IS THE HYDROSPHERE?

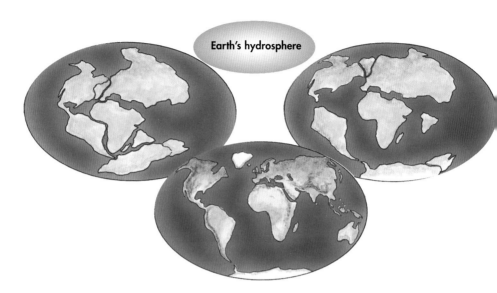

Earth's hydrosphere

All bodies of water and ice – as well as water in the atmosphere – make up the Earth's hydrosphere. The earth's surface is 71 per cent water – almost all of it in the oceans. The waters of the hydrosphere are important in many ways. Animals and plants need water to live. Plants use water to make food, and are eaten by human beings and animals. Water also wears away rocks and slowly turns them into soil that is necessary for growing crops. Oceans and other large bodies of water also help control the Earth's weather and climate. The temperature of water does not change as fast as that of land. Wind blowing over a large body of water can keep land from becoming extremely hot or extremely cold.

FACT FILE

All the Earth's animals and plants live on the Earth's surface or close to the surface – underground, underwater, or in the atmosphere. The region where life is found is called the earth's biosphere.

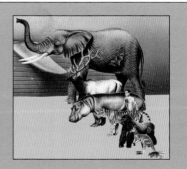

WHERE IS THE NATION OF IMMIGRANTS?

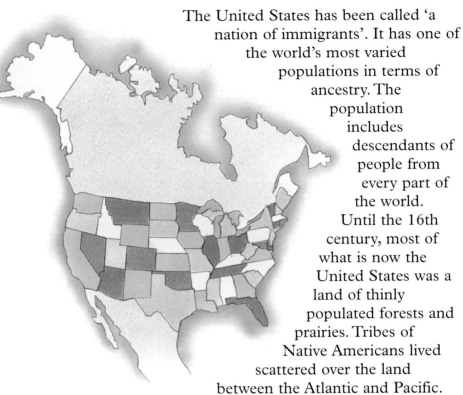

The United States has been called 'a nation of immigrants'. It has one of the world's most varied populations in terms of ancestry. The population includes descendants of people from every part of the world. Until the 16th century, most of what is now the United States was a land of thinly populated forests and prairies. Tribes of Native Americans lived scattered over the land between the Atlantic and Pacific. Inuits (also called Eskimos) inhabited what is now Alaska, and Polynesians lived in Hawaii. People in Europe saw in this vast 'new world' a chance to build new and better lives. Small groups of Spaniards settled in what is now the southeastern and western United States in the 16th century. People from England and some other European countries began settling along and near the East Coast during the 17th century. The United States is divided into 50 states and the District of Columbia.

FACT FILE

Covered wagons were used to carry people and supplies to the West before the coming of the railroad. They were known as prarie schooners.

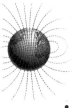

WHERE WOULD YOU SEE A STALACTITE?

Stalactites are seen in limestone caverns. They are icicle-shaped masses of calcite attached to the roof of the cave. Stalactites are mineral deposits that form in caves, sometimes collectively called dripstone. Ground water trickling through cracks in the roofs of such caverns contains dissolved calcium bicarbonate. When a drop of water comes into contact with the air of the cavern, some of the calcium bicarbonate is transformed into calcium carbonate which forms a ring of calcite on the roof of the cavern. As this process is repeated time and time again, the length and thickness of the stalactite is increased.

FACT FILE

A stalagmite is a cone of mineral deposit that rises from the floor of a cave. A useful way of remembering the difference between stalactites and stalagmites is to say: stalactites hang 'tite' to the ceiling while stalagmites hold with all their 'mite' to the floor!

WHERE IS THE BERMUDA TRIANGLE?

The Bermuda Triangle is an area between Florida's Fort Lauderdale, Bermuda and Puerto Rico, and covers about 1,140,000 square km (440,000 square miles). It is supposed to be the site of mysterious disappearances of ships and aircraft.

Despite the fact that there are no more disappearances here than anywhere else with similar weather conditions, numerous theories have been put forward, ranging from aliens to paranormal activity, as well as more plausible ideas such as sudden bad weather or pilot error.

A more recent theory is that large amounts of methane compounds caused by the decay of plants are stored in the sea floor of the American continental shelf and that if they are jolted by an earthquake they bubble up to the surface. If sufficient were released, they would make it impossible for the water to support the weight of a ship or for an aeroplane to stay in the sky.

FACT FILE

The first US ship to disappear in the triangle was the USS *Cyclops* in March 1918. On Dec. 5, 1945, a squadron of US bombers disappeared in bad weather, and a seaplane searching for the aircraft vanished, although there were reports of an explosion.

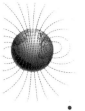

WHERE IS THE GOLDEN HORN?

Istanbul is the largest city in Turkey, although the capital is Ankara, several hundred kilometres to the east. The city lies to either side of the Bosphorus – between the Sea of Marmara and the Black Sea – and the Golden Horn is an inlet to the west of this strait. Around it lie the twin centres of Instanbul: to the south is Sultanahmet, the historical core of the city – where the Aya Sofia Mosque, the Topkapi Palace, the Blue Mosque and the 4,000 shops of the covered bazaar can be found – and to the north is Taksim, where the business district starts. The Golden Horn was an important harbour and twice during the city's long history, its capture led to the fall of the city.

FACT FILE

Between AD 330 and 1453, Istanbul was the capital of the eastern Roman empire and then the Byzantine empire. In the latter year, it fell to the armies of the Ottoman empire and became the centre of a magnificent Islamic empire.

Istanbul

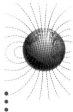

WHERE WAS THE ANCIENT CITY OF CARTHAGE?

FACT FILE

Thynes, a settlement on the site of present-day Tunis, was part of the ancient empire of Carthage. The settlement gradually developed into the city of Tunis.

Carthage was on the Mediterannean coast of what is now Tunisia, on the eastern side of Lake Tunis. According to legend, it was founded by Queen Dido in 814 BCE as an outpost of the Phoenician Empire, which was based in Tyre (now in southern Lebanon). Over the following centuries it became dominant in the western Mediterannean but as the Roman Empire grew in strength conflict became inevitable and Rome won all the three wars between them. In the first Punic War, Rome gained Sicily, then later annexed Sardinia and Corsica. In the second, Hannibal failed to regain territory while in the third, Rome destroyed the city of Carthage and took over the Carthaginian empire.

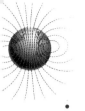

WHERE DO CACTI GROW IN THE WILD?

Cacti are native to North and South America and the West Indies, but now grow widely across the world, including Alaska and around the Mediterranean, where they spread after they were introduced to Spain following their conquest of South America.

What all cacti have in common is that they store water in their stems and have structures called areoles from which their spines, branches (if they have them) and flowers – which are adapted leaves – emerge.

Cacti come in many shapes and sizes from the branched opuntias and organ-pipe cacti, to the barrel-shape of mammilaria.

Not all cacti originate in deserts, some, such as the Christmas cactus, come from the rain forests of Brazil.

FACT FILE

Cacti have many rare and beautiful features. One of their principal characteristics is the ability to adapt to harsh conditions.

WHERE IS AUTUMN CALLED 'FALL'?

'Fall' is the term used in north America for autumn, because it is when the leaves fall from the trees. In some parts of the United States and Canada, such as New England, the autumn colours as the leaves of deciduous trees lose their green pigment before they fall are a major tourist attraction.

Trees lose their leaves and become dormant in order to survive the cold, dark days of winter. In warmer climates, such as the tropical rain forests, trees can retain their leaves all year, and so are called evergreens. In some cooler areas, trees such as pines have leaves adapted to withstand the cold.

FACT FILE

The peak time for hurricanes that affect the Gulf of Mexico and the west of the North Atlantic Ocean is August to September, although they can occur as early as May or as late as early January.

THE

HUMAN BODY

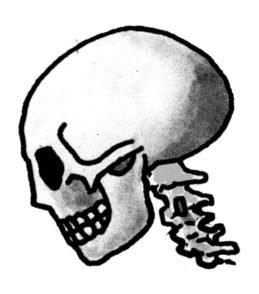

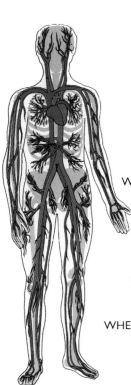

CONTENTS

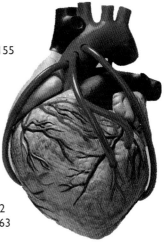

WHERE IS YOUR ACHILLES TENDON?

A tendon, also called a sinew, is a strong white cord that attaches muscles to bones and we have them all over our body. The Achilles tendon is the tendon at the back of the ankle. It attaches the muscles of the calf to the heel bone and is one of the stronger tendons in the body. The name Achilles tendon comes from the legend of Achilles, a Greek hero killed by an arrow in the heel.

The Achilles tendon may rupture as the result of a powerful upward movement of the foot or a blow to the calf when the calf muscles are contracted. This injury most commonly occurs in people over the age of thirty who compete in sports that involve running. Complete rupture is often accompanied by a snap, severe pain and the inability to push off or stand on the toes. As soon as possible, ice should be applied to the back of the ankle, and the leg should be raised and immobilized. Surgery may be needed to sew the tendon together. The person should keep their weight off the injured leg for up to two months before progressing to gradual stretching and strengthening exercises.

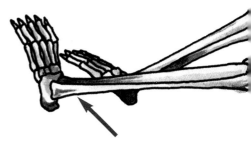

FACT FILE

Thirty-five powerful muscles move the human hand. Fifteen are in the forearm rather than in the hand itself. This arrangement gives great strength to the hand without making the fingers so thick with muscles that they would be difficult to move.

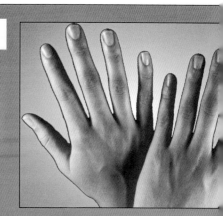

WHERE IS YOUR OCCIPITAL BONE?

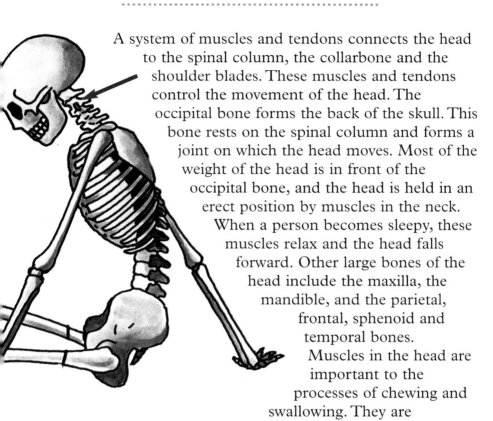

A system of muscles and tendons connects the head to the spinal column, the collarbone and the shoulder blades. These muscles and tendons control the movement of the head. The occipital bone forms the back of the skull. This bone rests on the spinal column and forms a joint on which the head moves. Most of the weight of the head is in front of the occipital bone, and the head is held in an erect position by muscles in the neck. When a person becomes sleepy, these muscles relax and the head falls forward. Other large bones of the head include the maxilla, the mandible, and the parietal, frontal, sphenoid and temporal bones. Muscles in the head are important to the processes of chewing and swallowing. They are responsible for facial expressions, such as smiling or frowning.

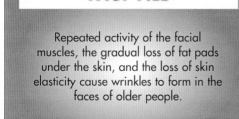

FACT FILE

Repeated activity of the facial muscles, the gradual loss of fat pads under the skin, and the loss of skin elasticity cause wrinkles to form in the faces of older people.

WHERE IS THE SMALLEST BONE IN YOUR BODY?

The smallest bone in the body is called the stirrup. It is in the middle ear and is part of the system that carries sound signals to the brain. At only 3 mm (⅛ inch) long, the stirrup is about the size of a grain of rice. The footplate of the stirrup bone is attached to a membrane called the oval window, which leads to the inner ear. It is connected to two other very small bones called the hammer and the anvil. All three of these bones are joined to the eardrum, where sound is collected before it is sent in the form of nerve signals to the brain.

The ear is a very important organ for keeping our sense of balance. Without a sense of balance, we could not hold our body steady, and we would stagger and fall when we tried to move.

FACT FILE

Some people suffer from motion sickness when they travel by boat, car, train or airplane. Motion sickness is caused by excessive stimulation of the vestibular organs. But researchers do not know why some people develop motion sickness more easily than others.

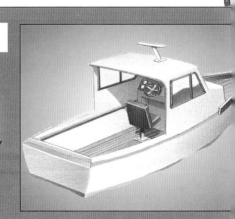

WHERE IS THE MANDIBLE?

There are fourteen bones in the face; the two that make up the jaw are the maxillae (upper jaw) and the mandible (lower jaw). The mandible, like the maxilla, contains sockets for the 32 teeth, which are embedded in fibrous tissue. Teeth are hard, bonelike structures in the upper and lower jaws of human beings and many kinds of animals. They are the hardest parts of the body.

Muscles in the head are important to the processes of chewing and swallowing. They are responsible for facial expressions, such as smiling or frowning. A system of muscles and tendons connects the head to the spinal column, the collarbone and the shoulder blades. These muscles and tendons control the movement of the head.

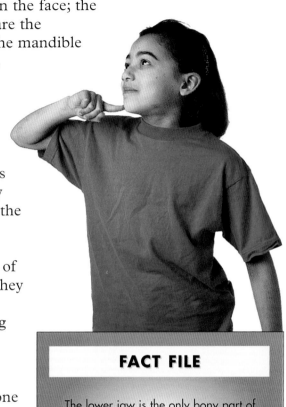

FACT FILE

The lower jaw is the only bony part of the face that moves. There are 32 permanent teeth, 16 in each jaw. Each jaw has 4 incisors, 2 canines, 4 premolars and 6 molars.

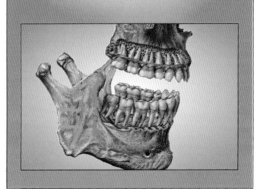

WHERE ARE YOUR ADENOIDS?

Pharyngeal tonsil (adenoid)

The adenoids, also known as pharyngeal tonsils, are a mass of glandlike tissue normally present in the upper part of the throat, directly behind the nasal passages. A small amount of this tissue is always found in the throats of newborn babies. Usually it shrinks gradually and disappears by the time the child is 10 years old. Sometimes this shrinking process does not take place; instead, the adenoid tissue increases in varying degrees to form a large growth. It is this growth that people commonly call 'adenoids'.

The adenoids form a continuous ring of lymphoid tissue around the back of the throat. If the adenoid tissue causes repeated infections, doctors may remove it in a surgical operation called an adenoidectomy.

FACT FILE

No one really knows the purpose of tonsils, but many medical scientists believe they aid in protecting the respiratory and digestive systems from infection. Tonsils consist of a type of tissue called lymphoid tissue. This tissue produces white blood cells, known as lymphocytes, that help fight infection.

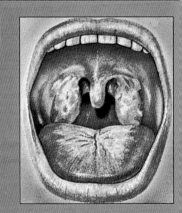

WHERE ARE YOUR VOCAL CORDS?

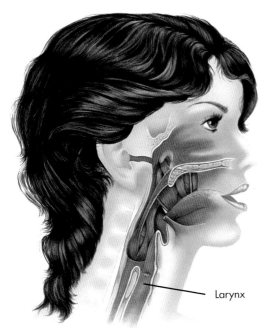

Larynx

The vocal cords are the main sound producers in human beings. These two small folds of tissue stretch across the larynx. The larynx is a section of the air passage in the throat. It is located between the back of the tongue and the trachea (windpipe). The larynx is sometimes called the voice box, because it contains the vocal cords. Muscles in the larynx stretch and relax the vocal cords. When we breathe, we relax our vocal cords so they form a V-shaped opening that lets air through. When we speak, we pull the vocal cords by the attached muscles, narrowing the opening. Then, as we drive air from the lungs through the larynx, the air vibrates the tightened vocal cords and sounds results. The more the cords are stretched, the higher are the sounds produced. The more relaxed the cords, the lower the sounds.

FACT FILE

The pitch of the voice is determined by the size of the larynx. Women's voices are usually pitched higher than men's because their vocal cords are shorter.

WHERE WOULD YOU FIND PAPILLAE?

FACT FILE

The sense of taste is the crudest of our five senses. It is limited in both range and versatility. Each papilla contains one to two hundred taste buds.

Papillae are found on the surface of your tongue. The chief organ of taste, the tongue also helps in chewing and swallowing, and plays an important part in forming the sounds of words. Covered with a mucous membrane, the undersurface of the tongue is smooth, but many papillae (small projections) give the top of the tongue a rough surface. There are four kinds of papillae: filiform, folioform and vallate, which are only found at the back of the tongue, and fungiform. The four types of taste buds, found in the papillae, enable us to distinguish between sweet, sour, salty and bitter tastes.

Epiglottis

Filiform papillae

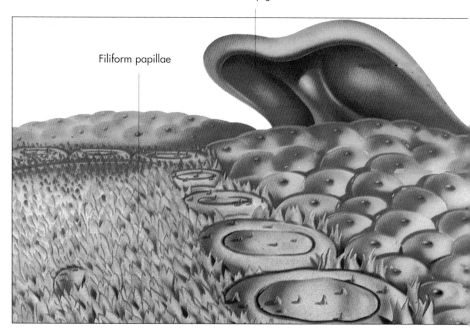

WHERE WOULD YOU FIND THE EPIGLOTTIS?

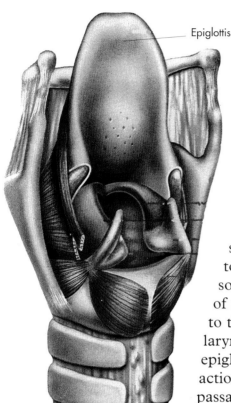

Epiglottis

The epiglottis is found in the throat. The throat is a term loosely applied to the part of the neck in front of the backbone. The throat contains structures important in breathing and eating. It includes the pharynx, the larynx, part of the oesophagus and part of the trachea.

Normally, when a person swallows, two actions take place to block off the air passage. The soft palate presses against the back of the pharynx, closing the opening to the nose. At the same time, the larynx rises and is covered by the epiglottis, a leaf-shaped lid. These actions force the food into its own passage, the oesophagus, and muscular waves carry it to the stomach.

FACT FILE

The thyroid is shaped like a bow tie under the skin of the neck. It manufactures three main hormones: calcitonin – which controls the level of calcium minerals in the blood and bones; thyroxine and tri-iodothyronine – which affect blood pressure and the speed of general body chemistry.

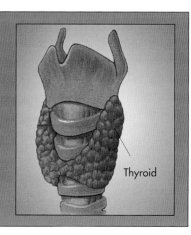

Thyroid

WHERE ARE THE ALVEOLI LOCATED?

The alveoli are located in the lungs. Human beings have two lungs – a left lung and a right lung – which fill up most of the chest cavity. A lung has a spongy texture and may be thought of as an elastic bag filled with millions of tiny air chambers called alveoli. If the walls of the alveoli could be spread out flat, they would cover about half a tennis court. The somewhat bullet-shaped lungs are suspended within the rib cage. They extend from just above the first rib down to the diaphragm, a muscular sheet that separates the chest cavity from the abdomen. A thin, tough membrane called the visceral pleura covers the outer surface of the lungs. The heart, large blood vessels and oesophagus (the tube connecting the mouth and stomach) lie between the two lungs.

Lungs

Heart   Rib cage

FACT FILE

Each alveolar duct in the lungs supplies about 20 alveoli. The very thin walls of each alveolus contain networks of extremely small blood vessels called pulmonary capillaries. Gas is exchanged between the blood in these capillaries and the gas in the alveoli.

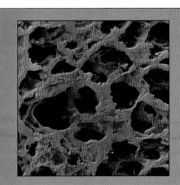

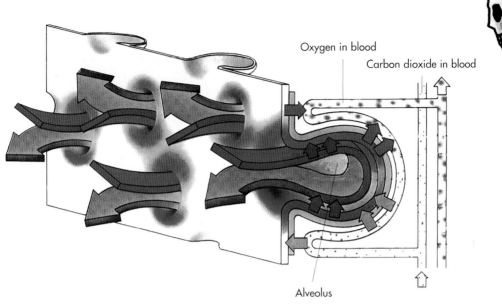

Oxygen in blood

Carbon dioxide in blood

Alveolus

WHERE DOES THE EXCHANGE OF GASES TAKE PLACE?

The exchange of gases takes place within the respiratory system.

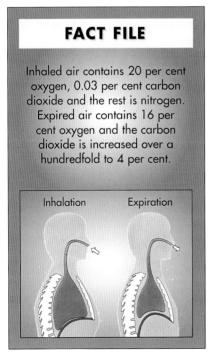

Inhalation   Expiration

The primary function of the respiratory system is to supply the blood with oxygen in order for the blood to deliver oxygen to all parts of the body. The respiratory system does this through breathing. When we breathe, we inhale oxygen and exhale carbon dioxide. This is known as the exchange of gases, and is the body's means of getting oxygen to the blood. Oxygen enters the respiratory system through the mouth and the nose. It is the job of the diaphragm to help pump the carbon dioxide out of the lungs and pull the oxygen into the lungs. The diaphragm is a sheet of muscles that lies across the bottom of the chest cavity.

WHERE IS SEROTONIN PRODUCED?

A group of cells in the base of the brain produce serotonin from an amino acid called L-tryptophan. Serotonin is also made in the digestive system and by certain skin and blood cells. Scientists have identified more than a dozen kinds of serotonin receptors in different areas of the body.

Serotonin is a chemical that acts in the brain and other parts of the body to influence many feelings, actions and processes. Some of the important functions regulated by serotonin include appetite, sleep, aggression and moods. In the brain and the rest of the nervous system, serotonin acts as a neurotransmitter, a chemical that carries signals from one nerve cell to another. In many cases, serotonin acts by modifying the effects of other neuro-transmitters. Serotonin also helps shape early brain development. Serotonin occurs widely in plants and in other animals as well as in human beings.

FACT FILE

Serotonin's many effects on the body make it a promising target for drugs. For example, drugs that raise serotonin levels in the nervous system are prescribed for treatment of depression, migraine headaches and schizophrenia.

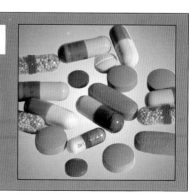

WHERE IS THE CEREBRUM?

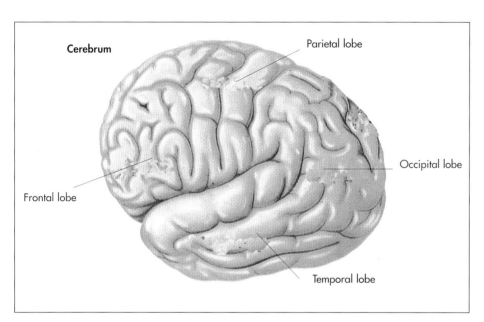

Cerebrum

Parietal lobe

Occipital lobe

Frontal lobe

Temporal lobe

FACT FILE

The brain stem is the vital control area of the brain and is concerned with maintaining all the essential regulatory mechanisms of the body: respiration, blood pressure, pulse rate, alertness and sleep.

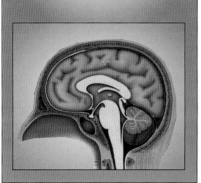

The cerebrum is in the brain and makes up about 85 per cent of its weight. A large groove called the longitudinal fissure divides the cerebrum into halves called the left cerebral hemisphere and the right cerebral hemisphere. The hemispheres are connected by bundles of nerves, the largest of which is the corpus callosum. Each hemisphere, in turn, is divided into four lobes. Each lobe has the same name as the bone of the skull that lies above it. The lobes are the frontal lobe, at the front; the temporal lobe, at the lower side; the parietal lobe, in the middle; and the occipital lobe, at the rear.

WHERE DOES DIGESTION START?

Digestion starts in the mouth. Chewing is very important for good digestion for two reasons. When chewed food is ground into fine particles, the digestive juices can act more easily. As the food is chewed, it is moistened and mixed with saliva, which contains the enzyme ptyalin. Ptyalin changes some of the starches in the food to sugar. After the food is swallowed, it passes through the oesophagus into the stomach. The digestive juice in the stomach is called gastric juice. It contains hydrochloric acid and the enzyme pepsin. This juice begins the digestion of protein foods such as meat, eggs and milk. Starches, sugars and fats are not digested by the gastric juice. After a meal, some food remains in the stomach for two to five hours.

FACT FILE

Almost no digestion occurs in the large intestine. The large intestine stores waste food products and absorbs water and small amounts of minerals. The waste materials that accumulate in the large intestine are roughage that cannot be digested in the body.

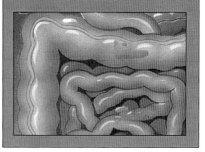

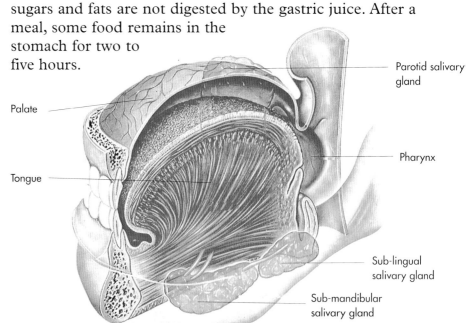

Parotid salivary gland

Palate

Pharynx

Tongue

Sub-lingual salivary gland

Sub-mandibular salivary gland

WHERE IS THE DIGESTIVE PROCESS COMPLETED?

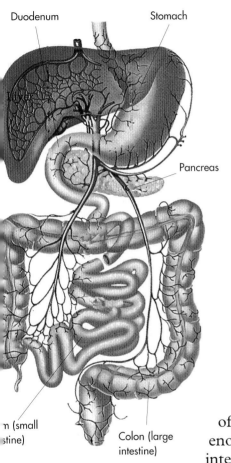

Duodenum

Stomach

Liver

Pancreas

n (small
stine)

Colon (large
intestine)

In the small intestine, the digestive process is completed on the partly digested food by pancreatic juice, intestinal juice and bile. The pancreatic juice is produced by the pancreas and pours into the small intestine through a tube, or duct. The intestinal juice is produced by the walls of the small intestine. It has milder digestive effects than the pancreatic juice, but carries out similar digestion. Bile is produced in the liver, stored in the gallbladder, and flows into the small intestine through the bile duct. When the food is completely digested, it is absorbed by tiny blood and lymph vessels in the walls of the small intestine. It is then carried into the circulation for nourishment of the body. Food particles are small enough to pass through the walls of the intestine and blood vessels only when they are completely digested.

FACT FILE

The small intestine is about 7 m (7.6 yards) long and is lined with small finger-like protuberances called villi. The successful absorption of nutrients depends on their transport away from the cells of the villi into the bloodstream.

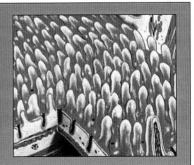

WHERE IS URINE STORED?

The bladder is the common name for the urinary bladder, a hollow muscular organ that stores urine before expelling it from the body. The emptying of the urinary bladder is voluntarily controlled in most human beings and many other mammals. The bladder lies just behind the pubis, one of the bones of the pelvis. Urine drains continuously from the kidneys into the bladder through two tubes called ureters. It leaves the bladder through the urethra, a wider tube that leads out of the body. The place where the bladder and the urethra meet is called the neck of the bladder. A complex arrangement of muscles encircles the bladder neck. This ring, called the urethral sphincter, normally prevents urine from leaving the bladder. The bladder can hold more than ½ litre (1 pint) of urine.

FACT FILE

We lose around 3 litres (5 pints) of water a day through our skin as sweat, and in our breath and urine. We also get rid of extra salt in sweat and we expel waste carbon dioxide gas when we breathe out.

Skin
Lungs

Kidneys

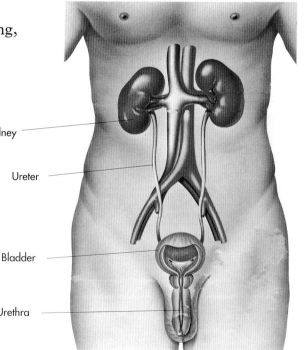

Kidney

Ureter

Bladder

Urethra

WHERE WOULD YOU FIND NEPHRONS?

Nephrons are found in the kidneys; they are millions of tiny filtering units. The renal artery brings unfiltered blood to the kidneys. It branches into over 1 million capillaries inside each kidney. Each capillary is twisted into a knot called the glomerulus which is enclosed by a structure called a Bowman's capsule. Blood is cleaned as it filters through the capsule and the tubule attached to it. Clean blood passes back into the capillaries which join up into the renal vein. Urine continues down the tubule, which joins up with other tubules to form the ureter leading to the bladder.

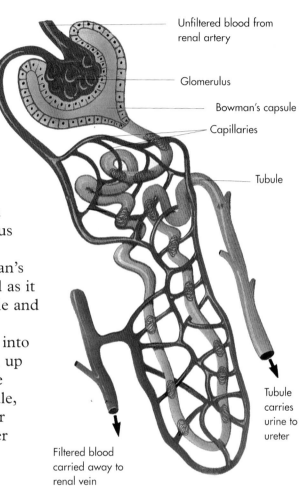

Unfiltered blood from renal artery

Glomerulus

Bowman's capsule

Capillaries

Tubule

Tubule carries urine to ureter

Filtered blood carried away to renal vein

FACT FILE

The two kidneys perform many vital functions, of which the most important is the production of urine. Two healthy kidneys contain a total of about 2 million nephrons, which filter about 1900 litres (500 gallons) of blood daily.

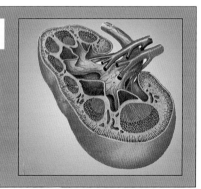

WHERE IS THE COCCYX SITUATED?

The coccyx is situated at the base of the spine. The axial skeleton is made up of the bones of the head, neck and trunk. The spine forms an axis that supports the other parts of the body. The skull is at the top of the spine. The spine consists of separate bones, called vertebrae, with fibrous discs between them. The ribs are attached to the thoracic vertebrae. There are usually 12 ribs on each side of the body; they protect the heart and lungs, and act as a bellows box for the breathing process.

    The five lumbar vertebrae lie in the lower part of the back. Below the last lumbar vertebra is the sacrum, followed by the coccyx. In children, four separate bones make up the coccyx. The three lowest of these bones often fuse together during adulthood to form a beak-like bone. The point where the sacrum and coccyx meet remains fibrous throughout life.

Coccyx

FACT FILE

The human foot has 26 bones. They are (1) the seven tarsals, or anklebones; (2) the five metatarsals, or instep bones; and (3) the 14 phalanges, or toe bones.

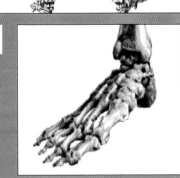

WHERE ARE THE METACARPALS?

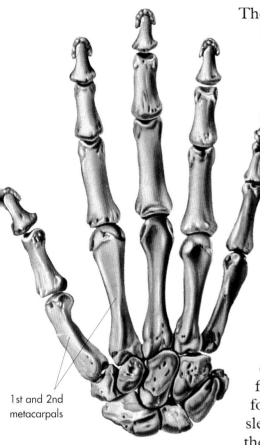

1st and 2nd metacarpals

The metacarpals are bones in the human hand. The hand consists of the carpals (wrist bones), the metacarpals (palm bones) and the phalanges (four fingers and thumb). There are 27 bones in the hand. Eight carpal bones make up the wrist. They are arranged roughly in two rows. In the row nearest the forearm, starting from the thumb side, are the scaphoid, lunate, triquetrum and pisiform bones. In the second row are the trapezium, trapezoid, capitate and hamate bones. Five long metacarpal bones make up the palm. They connect the wrist with the fingers and thumb. Each of the four fingers contains three slender phalanges. However, the thumb contains only two phalanges.

FACT FILE

Muscles can't push, they can only pull. Muscles are pulling gently against each other most of the time. This keeps them firm and stops them from becoming floppy. Muscles get bigger and stronger if you exercise them. Muscles are joined to bones by tough 'bands' called tendons.

WHERE ARE THE VERTEBRAE?

The vertebrae form a column of bones in the spine. The spine is the part of the skeleton that extends down the middle of the back. The spine plays an important role in posture and movement, and it also protects the spinal cord. The spine is also called the spinal column, vertebral column, or backbone.

The human spine consists of 33 vertebrae, but some of them grow together in adults. There are 7 cervical (neck), 12 thoracic (chest region), 5 lumbar (lower back), 5 sacral (hip region) and 4 coccygeal (tailbone region) vertebrae. The vertebrae are held in place by muscles and strong connective tissue called ligaments. Most vertebrae have fibrous intervertebral discs between them to absorb shock and enable the spine to bend. The spine normally has a slight natural curve.

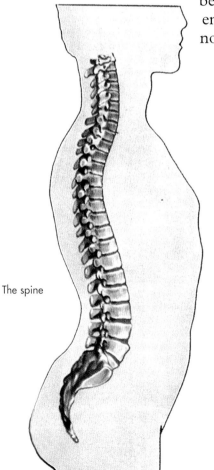

The spine

FACT FILE

Many people suffer from backaches. Sometimes the intervertebral disc, the tissue that lies between the vertebrae, sticks out and presses on nerves. This condition is called a slipped disc. It can cause severe pain in the lower back, thighs, and legs.

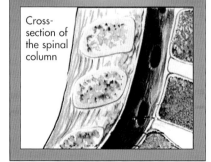

Cross-section of the spinal column

WHERE IS THE HUMERUS BONE?

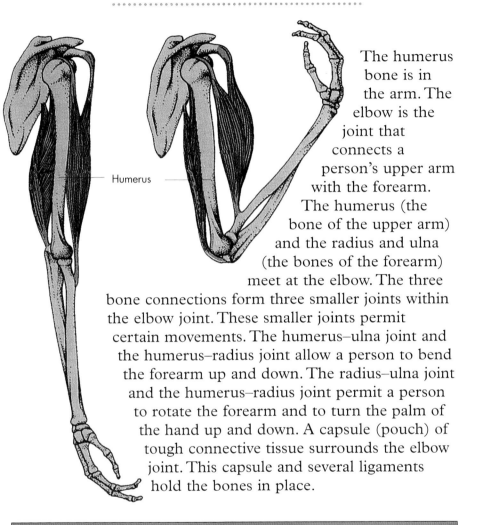

Humerus

The humerus bone is in the arm. The elbow is the joint that connects a person's upper arm with the forearm. The humerus (the bone of the upper arm) and the radius and ulna (the bones of the forearm) meet at the elbow. The three bone connections form three smaller joints within the elbow joint. These smaller joints permit certain movements. The humerus–ulna joint and the humerus–radius joint allow a person to bend the forearm up and down. The radius–ulna joint and the humerus–radius joint permit a person to rotate the forearm and to turn the palm of the hand up and down. A capsule (pouch) of tough connective tissue surrounds the elbow joint. This capsule and several ligaments hold the bones in place.

FACT FILE

Excessive or violent twisting of the forearm may injure the elbow ligaments, capsule, or tendons. One such injury, sometimes called tennis elbow, often results from playing tennis.

WHERE IS THE LARGEST JOINT IN THE BODY?

The knee joint is the largest and most complex joint in the body. The knee is the joint where the thighbone meets the large bone of the lower leg. The knee moves like a hinge, but it can also rotate and move a little from side to side. The knee is more likely to be damaged than most other joints because it is subject to tremendous forces during vigorous activity. Most of the knee injuries that occur in football and other sports result from twisting the joint. The knee ligaments are the strongest connections between the femur and the tibia. Ligaments keep the bones from moving out of position.

Patella

Tibia

Fibul

FACT FILE

The patella (or kneecap) is a small, flat, triangular bone in front of the joint. It is not directly connected with any other bone. Muscle attachments hold it in place.

Patella

WHERE IS THE LARGEST MUSCLE IN THE BODY?

The largest muscle in the human body is called the gluteus maximus and this is situated in the buttocks, while the smallest is the stapedius which can be found in the middle ear. A muscle is the tough, elastic tissue that makes body parts move. Muscles are found throughout the body. As a person grows, the muscles also get bigger. Muscle makes up nearly half the body weight of an adult. The human body has more than 600 major muscles and about 240 of them have specific names. There are two main types of muscles: (1) skeletal muscles and (2) smooth muscles. A third kind of muscle, called cardiac muscle, has characteristics of both skeletal and smooth muscles. It is found only in the heart. People use muscles to make various movements.

Gluteus
maximus

FACT FILE

Among the most powerful muscles are the masseters, one on each side of the face. The longest muscle is the sartorius, which runs from the side of the waist, diagonally down across the front of the thigh to the inside of the knee.

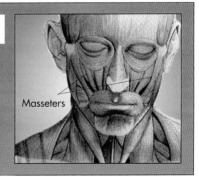

Masseters

WHERE IS OUR CIRCULATORY SYSTEM?

Heart

Arteries
(red)

Veins (blue)

The circulatory system is a network that carries blood throughout the body. The human circulatory system supplies the cells of the body with the food and oxygen they need to survive. At the same time, it carries carbon dioxide and other wastes away from the cells. The circulatory system also helps regulate the temperature of the body and carries substances that protect the body from disease. In addition, the system transports chemical substances called hormones, which help regulate the activities of various parts of the body. The blood vessels form a complicated system of connecting tubes throughout the body. There are three major types of these blood vessels. Arteries carry blood from the heart. Veins return blood to the heart. Capillaries are extremely tiny vessels that connect the arteries and the veins.

FACT FILE

The human circulatory system has three main parts: (1) the heart, (2) the blood vessels, and (3) the blood. A watery fluid called lymph, and the vessels that carry it, are sometimes considered a part of the circulatory system.

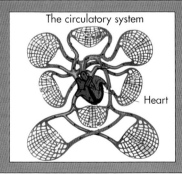

The circulatory system

Heart

WHERE ARE THE AORTIC AND PULMONIC VALVES?

Both sides of the heart pump blood at the same time. As the right ventricle contracts and sends blood to the lungs, the left ventricle also contracts and squeezes blood out to the body. The heart's cycle of activity has two stages, systole and diastole. Systole occurs when the ventricles contract. Diastole is the stage when the ventricles relax and the atria contract. One complete cycle of contraction and relaxation – called a cardiac cycle – makes up one heartbeat. During each cardiac cycle, the heart valves open and close. Closing of the valves produces most of the 'lub dub' sound of a heartbeat, which doctors can hear with an instrument called a stethoscope. As the ventricles contract, the mitral and tricuspid valves close, causing the first sound (1). Immediately after the valves close, pressure in the ventricles forces the aortic and pulmonic valves to open (2). After a contraction ends, pressure in the ventricles drops (3). The aortic and pulmonic valves then close, causing most of the second heart sound (4).

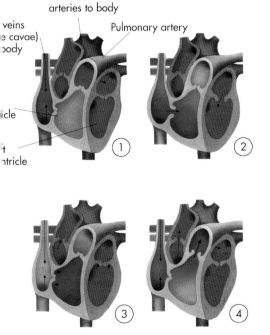

Aorta and main arteries to body

veins
e cavae)
body

Pulmonary artery

cle

t
tricle

(1) (2) (3) (4)

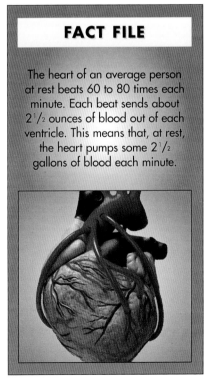

FACT FILE

The heart of an average person at rest beats 60 to 80 times each minute. Each beat sends about $2^1/_2$ ounces of blood out of each ventricle. This means that, at rest, the heart pumps some $2^1/_2$ gallons of blood each minute.

WHERE IS THE LARGEST GLAND IN THE BODY?

The liver is the largest gland in the human body and one of the most complex of all human organs. It serves as the body's main chemical factory and is one of its major storehouses of food. The liver is a reddish-brown mass weighing about 1.4 kg (3 pounds). It is located in the upper right part of the abdomen, under the diaphragm and above the stomach and intestines. The liver performs many essential functions. One of its most important tasks is to help the body digest food. The liver produces and discharges bile, a greenish-yellow digestive fluid. Bile travels from the liver to the small intestine, where it aids in the digestion of fats. Extra bile is stored in the gallbladder, a pear-shaped pouch that lies under the liver.

Hepatic valve

Liver

Stomach

Spleen

Gall bladder

Pancreas

FACT FILE

The liver has a remarkable ability to produce new cells to replace its own diseased or damaged cells. For example, surgeons can remove a section of a healthy liver from an adult and transplant it into a child who has a diseased liver. The child's new liver will grow as the child grows.

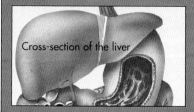

Cross-section of the liver

WHERE WOULD YOU USE A BRONCHOSCOPE?

A bronchoscope would be used to examine the trachea and the bronchial tubes of the lungs. It is an instrument consisting of a hollow tube with a system of lights and mirrors.

A bronchoscope is inserted through the patient's mouth or nose into the throat and lungs. It enables a physician to detect diseased areas that cannot be seen by X-rays. Attachments, such as a sucking needle, forceps, , and brush can be added to a bronchoscope. Physicians use them to remove small tumours, pus, foreign bodies and samples of lung tissue.

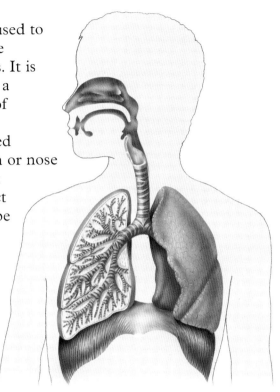

FACT FILE

Because the lungs must inhale the air from the environment, they are exposed to bacteria, viruses, dust and pollutants that are mixed with the air. A sticky fluid called mucus lines the airways and traps most of these foreign substances.

TELL ME WHERE : THE HUMAN BODY

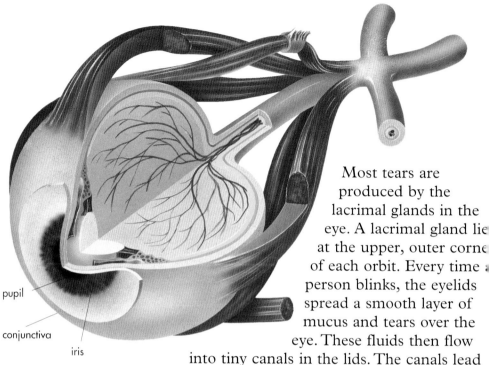

pupil

conjunctiva

iris

Most tears are produced by the lacrimal glands in the eye. A lacrimal gland lie at the upper, outer corne of each orbit. Every time a person blinks, the eyelids spread a smooth layer of mucus and tears over the eye. These fluids then flow into tiny canals in the lids. The canals lead the lacrimal sac, a pouch at the lower, inner corner of each orbit. From the lacrimal sac, the mucus and tears drain through a passage into the nose. After crying, a person may have to blow the nose to clear this drainage system of the excess amount of tears. The conjunctiva is a membrane that lines the inside of the eyelids and extends over the front of the white part of the eye. It produces mucus, a clear, slimy fluid that lubricates the eyeball. The conjunctiv also produces some tears, which help keep the eye clean.

FACT FILE

In the middle of the iris is a round opening called the pupil, which looks like a black circle. The size of the pupil regulates the amount of light that enters the eye. Two muscles in the iris automatically adjust the size of the pupil to the level of light.

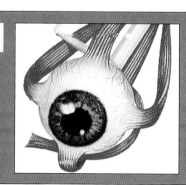

WHERE WOULD YOU FIND FOLLICLES?

You would find follicles at the root of an individual hair. A follicle is a long tunnel which reaches into the lower layers of the skin. At the end of the tiny tunnel, there is a hair papilla. The papilla is where most of the growth takes place, as it is here that nutrients are taken up from the blood.

Slightly below the surface of the skin there are sebaceous glands which supply the hair with sufficient sebum, the fatty secretion of these glands. A tiny hair-raising muscle is responsible for providing sebum from the sebaceous glands.

FACT FILE

A nail has three parts, the matrix, the plate and the bed. The matrix lies under the surface of the skin at the base of the nail. Most of the matrix is covered by skin.

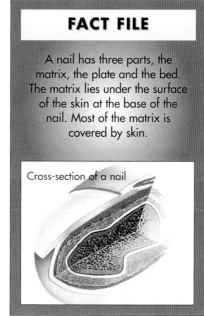

Cross-section of a nail

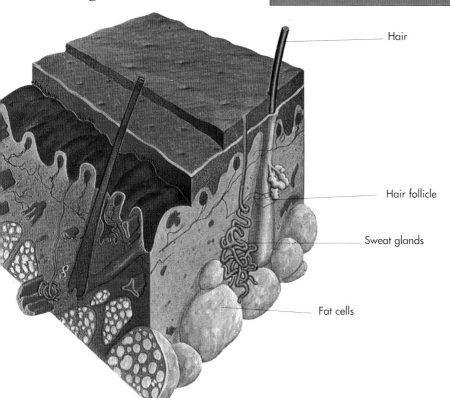

Hair

Hair follicle

Sweat glands

Fat cells

WHERE IS SPERM PRODUCED?

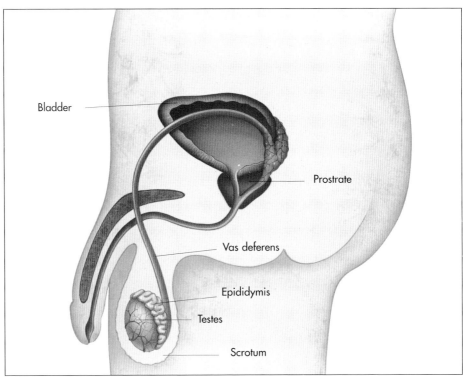

Bladder

Prostrate

Vas deferens

Epididymis

Testes

Scrotum

Sperm, the male sex cells, develop in the testes. It is stored for several days until needed. The testes contain long tubes called the seminiferous tubules, which are tightly coiled. Sperm is produced continuously in these tubes, then passed to the epididymis and stored in a large duct called the vas deferens. Here liquid is added to the sperm to make a milky fluid called semen. It is stored in pouches called seminal vesicles. During sexual intercourse the seminal vesicles contract and force out the sperm.

FACT FILE

Up to 100 million sperms are produced every day by the male. If they are not released they are soon destroyed and replaced. Sperms look like tiny tadpoles with rounded heads and long lashing tails.

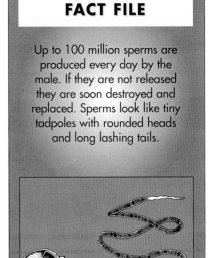

WHERE DOES MENSTRUATION TAKE PLACE?

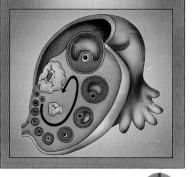

Menstruation, the loss of blood and cells that occurs about once a month in most women of child-bearing age, takes place through the vagina. During each month, blood and cells build up in the lining of a woman's uterus (or womb), a hollow, pear-shaped organ that holds a baby during pregnancy. The thickening of the lining prepares the uterus for pregnancy. If pregnancy does not occur, the lining breaks down. The blood and cells are discharged through the vagina, which is a canal that leads from the uterus to the outside of the body. The process of menstruation lasts from three to seven days, and this period of time is called the menstrual period.

The lining of the womb is shed as blood and tissue

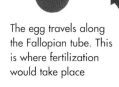

e unfertilized g passes into e womb

The egg travels along the Fallopian tube. This is where fertilization would take place

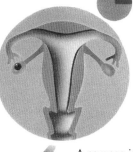

A new egg is released by the ovary

WHERE DOES A BABY DEVELOP?

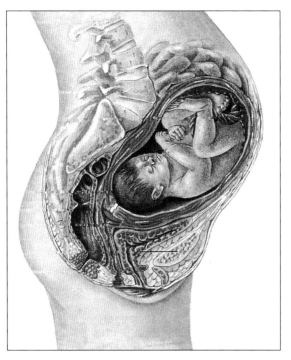

A baby develops in the uterus, or womb – a hollow, muscular organ in the mother's abdomen. The period of development in the uterus lasts about nine months in most cases. During this period, development is more rapid than at any time after birth.

For a baby to develop, a sperm from the father must unite with an egg from the mother. This union of a sperm and an egg is called fertilization. It produces a single cell called a fertilized egg. By a series of remarkable changes, the fertilized egg gradually develops into a baby.

FACT FILE

The placenta is an organ composed largely of blood vessels. The placenta is attached to the wall of the uterus. A tubelike structure called the umbilical cord joins the placenta to the embryo at the abdomen. The placenta supplies everything that the embryo needs to live and grow.

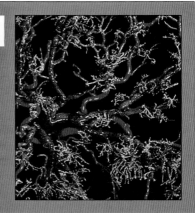

WHERE DOES LANUGO FORM ON A FOETUS?

By the fifth month of pregnancy, fine hair called lanugo covers the body of the foetus. Lanugo disappears late in pregnancy or shortly after birth. Hair also appears on the head.

From the ninth week of pregnancy until birth, the developing baby is called a foetus. In the first three months of this period, the foetus increases rapidly in length. It grows about 5 cm (2 inches) in each of these months. In the later months of pregnancy, the most striking change in the foetus is in its weight. Most foetuses gain about 700 grams (25 ounces) in both the eighth and ninth months of pregnancy. The mother can feel movements of the foetus by the fifth month of pregnancy. The eyelids open by the 26th week of pregnancy. By the 28th week, the fingernails and toenails are well developed. Until the 30th week, the foetus appears reddish and transparent because of the thinness of its skin and a lack of fat beneath the skin. In the last six to eight weeks before birth, fat develops rapidly and the foetus becomes smooth and plump.

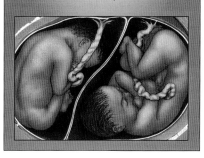

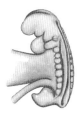

3-week embryo

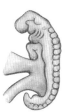

4-week embryo

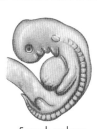

5-week embryo

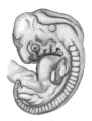

6-week embryo

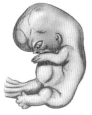

7-week embryo

8-week embryo

SCIENCE

AND SPACE

CONTENTS

• • • • • • • • • • • • • • • • • •

WHERE WOULD SOOT BE HARMFUL?

Soot can be harmful to the respiratory system, particularly the lungs. Soot is a black or dark brown substance found in smoke, and mainly consists of carbon particles. These particles have a diameter less than the width of a human hair. They form when carbon-containing fuels, such as coal, wood or oil, do not burn completely. Airborne soot is a form of air pollution. It sticks to any surface it touches. It can also cause widespread damage to property. Smoke blowing through a city leaves soot on buildings, making them look dingy. This soot can eventually damage the surfaces of the buildings by chemically reacting with them.

FACT FILE

Although soot can be a pollutant, it is also valuable as a pigment. Two kinds of soot used as pigments are bister and lampblack.

WHERE WOULD YOU USE A CATALYTIC CONVERTER?

A catalytic converter is a device that reduces the exhaust pollutants produced by a motor vehicle engine. The engine's combustion process gives off carbon monoxide and other harmful chemical compounds. A substance called a catalyst in the converter helps change these pollutants into safer substances. The catalyst in most converters is a blend of the metals platinum, palladium and rhodium.

The catalytic converter is installed in an automobile's exhaust system. As the exhaust gases pass through the converter, the catalyst causes carbon monoxide and other pollutants to change to oxygen, nitrogen, water and carbon dioxide.

FACT FILE

Cars with catalytic converters must use fuel that is free of both lead and phosphorus. These substances coat the catalyst's surface, making it ineffective.

WHERE WOULD YOU FIND CARBON?

Carbon is found in all living things: it is one of the most familiar and important chemical elements yet it makes up only 0.032 per cent of the earth's crust. Carbon is the main component of such fuels as coal, petroleum and natural gas. Carbon is also found in most plastics, many of which are derived from carbon fuels. Carbon has the chemical symbol C. Pure carbon occurs in four forms: (1) diamond (2) graphite (as used in pencils) (3) amorphous carbons and (4) fullerenes. The four forms have different crystalline structures – that is, their atoms are arranged differently. The various forms of carbon differ greatly in hardness and other properties, depending on how their atoms are arranged.

FACT FILE

Diamond is the hardest naturally occurring substance and one of the most valuable. Natural diamonds form in the rock beneath the Earth's crust where high temperature and pressure cause carbon atoms to make strong bonds with four other carbon atoms each and to crystallize.

WHERE WOULD YOU USE A CARBON TRANSMITTER?

A carbon transmitter is found in the handset of a landline telephone. It is a microphone, which produces an electric copy of the user's voice, and a receiver, which duplicates the voice of the person on the other end of the line. Mobile phones are two-way radios that convert the sound to radio waves, which travel through the air until they reach a receiver at a nearby base station. The base station sends your call through the network until it reaches the person you are calling. When you get a call, a nearby base station sends out radio waves that are detected by your mobile, where the signals are converted into voice or data.

FACT FILE

Alexander Graham Bell (1847–1922), a Scottish-born inventor and educator, is best known for his invention of the telephone. Bell was 27 years old when he worked out the principle of transmitting speech electrically, and was 29 when his basic telephone patent was granted in 1876.

WHERE WOULD YOU USE THERMOPLASTICS?

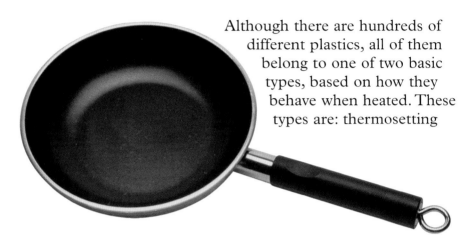

Although there are hundreds of different plastics, all of them belong to one of two basic types, based on how they behave when heated. These types are: thermosetting

plastics and thermoplastics. Thermoplastics can be melted and re-formed again and again. Their polymer chains do not form cross-links. So, the chains can move freely each time the plastic material is heated.

Thermoplastics are widely used because they are easier to handle. They also require less time to set – as little as 10 seconds. Thermoplastics can be dispersed in liquids to produce durable, high-gloss paints and lacquers. Because their molecules can slide slowly past one another, some thermoplastics tend to lose their shape when exposed to constant pressure over a long period of time. Polytetrafluoroethylene is a thermoplastic which resists heat and chemicals and slides easily. It is used for cable insulation, bearings, valve seats, gaskets, frying pan coatings, slides and cams.

FACT FILE

Products made from thermosetting plastics include pot handles, trays for sterilizing medical instruments and parts for airplanes and spacecraft.

WHERE DO RECYCLED GOODS COME FROM?

Recycled goods come from everyday waste, including cans, glass containers, newspapers and office paper. Recycling is a process designed to collect, process and reuse materials instead of throwing them away. Recycling programmes also collect plastics and used motor oil. Recycling helps conserve raw materials and energy that manufacturers would otherwise use to make new products. Recycling keeps materials out of landfills (areas where wastes are deposited and covered with earth or other material), saving scarce landfill space. Recycling also helps reduce the pollution that may result from waste disposal.

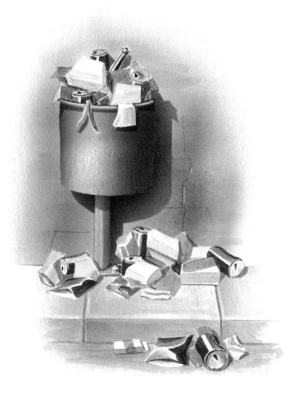

FACT FILE

When you buy a new car it may not be quite as new as you think. Up to 40 per cent of the steel may have come from old cars. Recycling scrap steel saves raw materials and energy.

WHERE WOULD YOU USE A BUNSEN BURNER?

A Bunsen burner is a gas burner used for heating substances in scientific laboratories. It consists of a metal tube on a stand and a long rubber hose that connects the tube to a gas jet. Several adjustable openings at the bottom of the tube control the amount of air that enters and mixes with the gas. The temperature of the flame is regulated by increasing or decreasing the amount of air in the tube. Because the gas mixes with air before burning, it produces a smokeless flame.

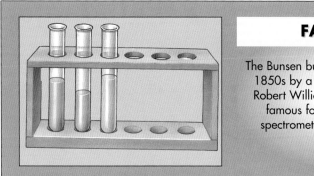

FACT FILE

The Bunsen burner was invented in the 1850s by a German chemist called Robert William Bunsen. He became famous for his work in using a spectrometer to identify chemical elements.

WHERE WOULD YOU SEE RUST?

Rust is a brownish-red substance that forms on the surface of iron or steel when it is exposed to damp air. The term used alone means iron rust, which consists mainly of hydrated iron oxide. Rust is formed by the union of oxygen in the air with iron by a process called oxidation.

Rust not only corrodes the surface but also weakens the metal. Long exposure to air and moisture will cause nails to rust off, and rust holes to form in sheet iron. Iron can be mixed with other chemical elements to create rust-resistant metals called stainless steels. Iron and steel that are not rust resistant should be kept dry or coated with a substance, such as chrome or paint, that will resist the action of oxygen. Polished tools may be easily protected if wiped with a cloth soaked in oil. Coating metal objects with heavy greases or spray-on plastics, or wrapping them in special chemically treated paper, also prevents rust.

FACT FILE

You would not want to eat with rusty cutlery, so chromium is added to steel to make an alloy called stainless steel. Unlike other metals, stainless steel will not react with acids in foods.

WHERE DID THEY USE A SURGICAL TREATMENT CALLED TREPHINING?

In prehistoric times the first known surgical treatment was an operation called trephining. People believed that angry gods or evil spirits caused disease. Curing the sick required calming the gods or driving the evil spirits from the body. The priests who tried to soothe the gods or drive out the evil spirits became the first professional healers of the sick.

Trephining (also known as trepanning) involved using a stone instrument to cut a hole in a patient's skull. Scientists have found fossils of trephined skulls as much as 10,000 years old. Early people may have performed the operation to release spirits believed responsible for headaches, mental illness, or epilepsy. Trephining may have brought relief in some cases by releasing pressure in the head. Surgeons still use a similar procedure to relieve some types of pressure on the brain.

FACT FILE

Prehistoric people probably also discovered that many plants can be used as drugs. For example, the use of quinine to prevent an illness called malaria. It is made from the bark of the cinchona tree.

WHERE WAS GLASS FIRST USED?

FACT FILE

It is very easy to recycle glass. It is simply broken up and melted, before being shaped again in the normal way.

Glass was probably first used as a glaze on pottery to waterproof it, but the first glass vessels were made in about 1500 BCE in Mesopotamia (modern Iraq) and Egypt. Bits of highly decorative glass vessels have been found in some tombs in the Valley of the Kings in Egypt, including a late fifteenth-century BCE bottle in the tomb of Amenhopis II. At this time glass vessels were formed around a core that was then removed as the technique of blowing glass had not been invented. The Egyptians also used coloured glass inlays on the coffins and mummy cases of pharoahs and other important people, as can be seen on the gold mask of Tutankhamun.

The Romans learned how to make blow pipes, and so blown glass, in about 30 BCE, which made glass vessels both easier and cheaper to manufacture.

Interestingly, although it appears solid, glass is, in fact, a liquid that has been cooled very quickly to prevent it forming crystals. It moves very slowly, but glass windows that are very old are thicker at the bottom because gravity has gradually pulled the glass down.

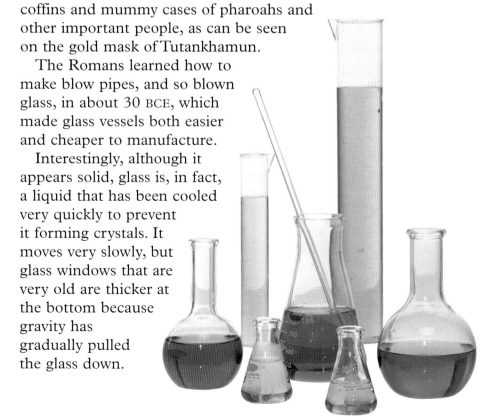

WHERE DOES THE WORD 'RADAR' COME FROM?

The word 'radar' comes from **ra**dio **d**etection **a**nd **r**anging. Radar is a scientific method used to detect and locate moving or fixed objects. Radar can determine the direction, distance, height and speed of objects that are much too far away for the human eye to see. It can find objects as small as insects or as large as mountains. Radar can even operate well at night and in heavy fog, rain or snow.

Almost every radar set works by sending radio waves towards an object and receiving the waves that are reflected from the object. The time it takes for the reflected waves to return indicates the object's range – how far away it is. The direction from which the reflected waves return tells the object's location.

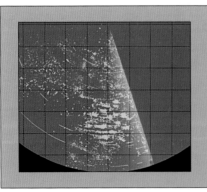

FACT FILE

Radar uses microwave radiation to detect distant objects. The microwaves usually scan round in a circle, and the echoes sent back produce an image on a screen.

WHERE WOULD YOU NEED GEARS?

A gear is a mechanical device that transfers rotating motion and power from one part of a machine to another. Gears are produced in a wide range of sizes, and they vary greatly in use. They range from the tiny gears that drive the hands of a watch to the huge gears that turn the propeller of a supertanker. A simple gear consists of a metal wheel or disc with slots called teeth around the edge. Gears always work in pairs. The teeth of one gear mesh (fit together) with the teeth of the other gear. Each gear has a metal axle in the middle. The axle of one gear is connected to a power source, such as an electric motor. When the power axle turns, its gear turns and causes the second gear to rotate in the opposite direction. This action powers the axle of the second gear to do useful work.

FACT FILE

A bicycle's gear system makes pedalling easier at certain times. Low gears, which make it easy to pedal up hills or against the wind, rotate the rear wheel only a little bit during each turn of the pedals.

WHERE DOES NITRIC ACID OCCUR NATURALLY?

Large quantities of nitric acid are produced naturally during thunderstorms and fall to the earth in rain. The rain falls as a very weak solution of nitric acid. The production of nitric acid during thunderstorms allows nitrogen from the air to become part of the soil in a form that plants can use. Nitric acid was one of the first acids known. Many alchemists of the Middle Ages used it in their experiments. Nitric acid is a strong inorganic acid that has many industrial uses. Its principal use is for the production of fertilizers and explosives.

FACT FILE

Nitric acid is such a powerful oxidizing agent that it dissolves many metals. But it does not attack gold and platinum. A drop of nitric acid on a ring or brooch tells whether it is made of genuine gold or platinum.

WHERE WAS THE FIRST LOCK FOUND?

The oldest key-operated lock still in existence was found in the citadel of King Sargon II. The citadel was built in the Assyrian capital of Khorsabad in the late 8th century BCE Similar locks are shown in Egyptian art dating from about 2000 BCE. These large wooden locks had bolts with pegs that served as simple pin-tumblers. A matching wooden key raised the tumblers and released the bolt.

The ancient Romans developed the first warded locks, which remained the most common locks until the 19th century. These locks have several fixed ridges or obstacles called wards that stop the wrong key from operating the lock. The correct key has notches cut into it that match the wards inside the lock. When a person inserts the correct key, the key fits past the wards and moves a spring inside the lock. The spring is attached to a bolt or shackle – the curved part of a padlock that snaps into the padlock's body. When the spring moves, the bolt or shackle slides to a locked or unlocked position.

FACT FILE

Tumbler locks have movable metal parts called tumblers that prevent the wrong key from opening the lock. Because tumblers provide more security than wards, most door locks use some type of tumbler arrangement.

WHERE WAS THE FIRST ANAESTHETIC USED?

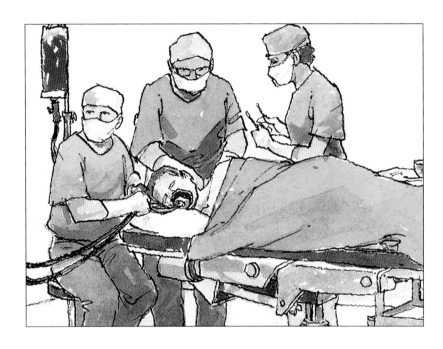

For thousands of years, physicians tried to dull pain during surgery by administering alcoholic drinks, opium and various other drugs. But no drug had proved really effective in reducing the pain and shock of operations. Then, in the 1840s, two Americans – Crawford Long and William T. G. Morton – discovered that ether gas could safely put patients to sleep during surgery. Long, a physician, and Morton, a dentist, appear to have made the discovery independently. With an anaesthetic, doctors could perform many operations that they could not attempt on conscious patients.

FACT FILE

With its pliers and saw, this box looks rather like a tool box. In fact, it was a surgeon's case used during the American Civil War.

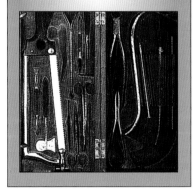

WHERE DOES HELIUM COME FROM?

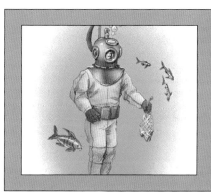

On the Earth, helium comes from natural gas deposits in the atmosphere. The atmosphere contains about 5 parts of helium per million parts of air. Helium is a lightweight gas and chemical element and makes up only a small fraction of the Earth's matter. But it is one of the most common elements in the universe. The Sun and other stars are made mostly of helium and hydrogen. The energy of these stars is produced when hydrogen atoms join together to form helium atoms. Because helium is so light, it constantly escapes from the atmosphere and drifts into space. But the lost helium is replaced by radioactive

minerals that shoot out alpha particles. Helium is also used to fill scientific balloons. The balloons rise to high altitudes, because helium is lighter than air. In air, helium has 92 per cent of the lifting ability of hydrogen. It is safer than hydrogen because it will not burn, as hydrogen will.

FACT FILE

Divers sometimes breathe a mixture of helium and oxygen to avoid a painful illness called nitrogen narcosis. Nitrogen narcosis usually occurs at depths below 30 metres (100 feet).

WHERE DID THE IDEA OF THE LAVA LAMP COME FROM?

Edward Craven Walker was a native of Singapore who flew reconnaissance missions for the Royal Air Force. One day, while visiting a pub in Hampshire, England, he became fascinated by an egg-timer on a shelf behind the bar. The timer was essentially a blob of solid wax suspended in a clear liquid in a cocktail shaker. Drop the shaker into boiling water with an egg and when the wax melted and floated to the top, the egg was done. As Walker looked at the egg timer, he saw the lava lamp.

He sought the inventor of the egg timer and discovered that he had died without patenting it, so Walker spent the better part of the next 15 years perfecting a way to mass-produce his 'astro lamp'. The theory behind his novelty lamp was relatively simple – enclose two liquids which are similar in density and insoluble in one another and apply heat. The most common insoluble liquids are oil and water. However, the oil is nowhere near dense enough to achieve the desired result. What chemicals did Walker use? The recipe is a trade secret, only the manufacturers of lava lamps know the exact ingredients.

FACT FILE

This strange lamp was an immediate hit in the psychedelic 1960s. Soon more than seven million lava lamps were being sold each year. Just as quickly, the fad ended.

WHERE WOULD YOU USE A MICROSCOPE?

A microscope is an instrument used to enlarge the image of a small item so that it can more easily be studied. The simplest form is a magnifying glass, with a single lens, but what we think of as a microscope has two lenses. The first one is thought to have been invented in about 1590, but it was only in the mid-nineteenth century that good-enough glass could be manufactured for the high-quality lenses needed to make the compound microscope a practical instrument to use.

They have many uses, including in medical laboratories and schools, by geologists to examine the fine detail of rock or fossils and by forensic scientists looking for clues about crimes.

To examine really minute particles, almost as small as atoms, biologists use scanning electron microsopes.

FACT FILE

Medical specialists use microscopes to look for the causes of diseases, such as viruses, bacteria and the abnormal cells present in such conditions as sickle-cell anaemia and cancer.

WHERE WERE THE FIRST GLASSES WORN?

Spectacles were probably first worn in Europe in the late thirteenth century and may have been brought back from China by Marco Polo, although there are possible references in literature that date back as far as 1235. Early lenses were convex (thicker in the middle) and corrected farsightedness, which prevents people focusing on objects nearby. In the fifteenth century, concave lenses (thinner in the middle) were first used to correct nearsightedness, in which distant objects are blurred. In the eighteenth century, Benjamin Franklin invented bifocals, which corrected both problems.

FACT FILE

Sunglasses have tinted glass or plastic lenses that reduce the amount of light entering the eye and therefore the risk of eye damage. Looking at the Sun can damage the eyes, so it is important not to do so.

WHERE WOULD YOU FIND A TRANSISTOR?

A transistor is a tiny device that controls the flow of electric current and is found in radios, television sets, computers and almost every other kind of electronic equipment. Transistors vary in size tremendously.

Transistors replaced electronic components called vacuum tubes almost completely in the 1950s and 1960s because they have a number of advantages over vacuum tubes. For example, transistors are smaller, lighter, less expensive to produce, cheaper to operate, and more reliable than vacuum tubes. Transistors are the main components built into computer chips. Some chips no larger than a fingernail contain millions of transistors. A transistor has two basic functions: (1) to switch electric current on and off and (2) to amplify or strengthen electric current.

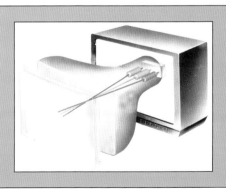

FACT FILE

The ability to amplify signals makes transistors essential parts of radios and television sets. The broadcast waves that travel through the air generate weak currents in a radio or TV antenna. Transistors amplify these signals to produce sounds and pictures.

WHERE IS METAMORPHIC ROCK FOUND?

Metamorphic rock is found in the Earth's crust along with two other kinds of rock: igneous and sedimentary. Igneous rocks are formed when melted rock deep inside the Earth's crust cools and hardens – or erupts at the surface as lava. Sedimentary rocks develop from materials that once were part of older rocks or of plants or animals. These materials were worn away from the land. They then collected in low places, layer upon layer, and hardened into rock. Many sedimentary rocks contain shells, bones and other remains of living things. Such remains, or the impressions of remains in sedimentary rocks, are called fossils. Metamorphic rocks are formed deep in the crust when igneous and sedimentary rocks are changed by heat and the weight of the Earth's crust presses on them.

FACT FILE

The Earth's crust is moving all the time, and here you can see the land has been pushed into giant folds.

WHERE IS THE MANTLE?

Beneath the Earth's crust is a sphere of hot rock and metal. By studying the records of earthquake waves, scientists have learned that the inside of the Earth is divided into three parts: the mantle, the outer core and the inner core.

The mantle is a thick layer of rock below the crust. It goes down about 2,900 km (1,800 miles). The rock in the mantle is made of silicon, oxygen, aluminium, iron and magnesium. The uppermost part of the mantle has a temperature of about 870°C (1600°F). The temperature gradually increases to about 4400°C (8000°F) in the deepest part of the mantle. The outer core begins about 2,900 km (1,800 miles) below the Earth's surface. The ball-shaped inner core lies within the outer core and makes up the middle of the Earth.

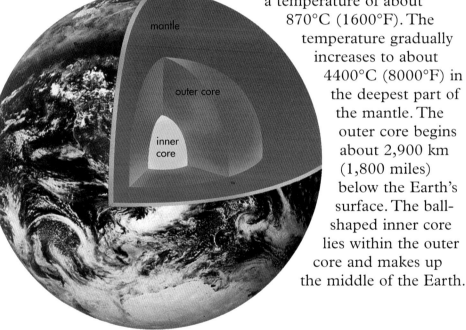

mantle

outer core

inner core

FACT FILE

The inner core rotates more rapidly than the remainder of the planet. During a period of about 400 years, the inner core rotates around the Earth's axis one more time than the surface does.

WHERE IS CALLISTO?

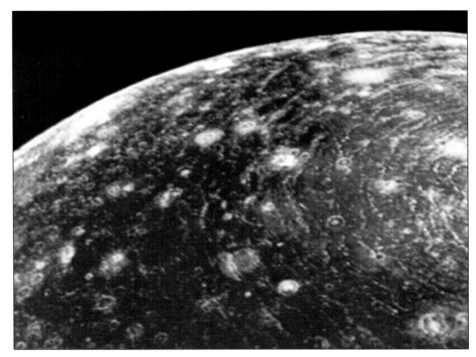

Callisto is a moon of Jupiter, which is bigger than the dwarf planet Pluto and almost as large as Mercury. It is one of the most heavily cratered bodies in the solar system. Its surface is covered with craters of all sizes caused by the impact of asteroids and comets. More than 4 billion years of bombardment have darkened Callisto's icy surface. The biggest impacts cracked the surface to form huge bull's-eye patterns. The surface is blanketed by dark dirt that accumulated when icy crater rims and cliffs crumbled away. This satellite has a carbon dioxide atmosphere that is only slightly denser than the near-vacuum of outer space.

FACT FILE

Callisto has a diameter of 4,806 km (2,986 mi). It orbits Jupiter every 16.7 days at a distance of 1,883,000 km (1,170,000 mi). The Italian astronomer Galileo discovered Callisto in 1610.

WHERE IS THERE A MOON OF ICE?

Europa is a large moon of Jupiter. Its surface is made of ice, which may have an ocean of water beneath it. Such an ocean could provide a home for living things. The surface layer of ice or ice and water is 80 to 160 km (50 to 100 miles) deep. The satellite has an extremely thin atmosphere. Electrically charged particles from Jupiter's radiation belts continuously bombard Europa.

Europa is one of the smoothest bodies in the solar system. Its surface features include shallow cracks, valleys, ridges, pits, blisters and icy flows. None of them extend more than a few hundred yards upwards or downwards. In some places, huge sections of the surface have split apart and separated. The surface of Europa has few impact craters. The splitting and shifting of the surface and disruptions from below have destroyed most of the old craters.

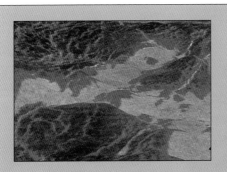

FACT FILE

Europa's interior is hotter than its surface. This internal heat comes from the gravitational forces of Jupiter and Jupiter's other large satellites, which pull Europa's interior in different directions.

WHERE DO ASTEROIDS COME FROM?

An asteroid is any of numerous small planetary bodies that revolve around the Sun. Asteroids are also called minor planets or planetoids. Most of them are located in the asteroid belt between the orbits of Mars and Jupiter. The belt contains more than 1,150 asteroids with diameters greater than 30 km (18 miles). Astronomers are not sure how the asteroids originated. According to the leading theory, however, most known asteroids are the shattered remains of a smaller group of larger objects. These objects were left over from the time the planets formed.

FACT FILE

Most asteroids drift harmlessly in their orbits around the Sun for billions of years. Occasionally, however, an asteroid may be knocked out of its orbit and sent on a collision course with a planet.

WHERE IS THERE A GIANT BALL OF GAS?

FACT FILE

The force of gravity at the surface of Jupiter is up to 2.4 times stronger than on Earth. So, an object that weighs 100 pounds on Earth would weigh as much as 240 pounds on Jupiter.

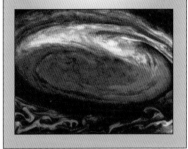

Jupiter, the largest planet in the solar system, is a giant ball of gas and liquid with little, if any, solid surface. Its diameter is 142,984 km (88,846 miles), more than 11 times that of Earth, and about one-tenth that of the Sun. The planet's surface is composed of dense red, brown, yellow and white clouds.

In 1995 the Galileo probe dropped a smaller probe into the turbulent atmosphere of the gas giant. It took measurements for 57 minutes before it was destroyed by Jupiter's atmospheric pressure.

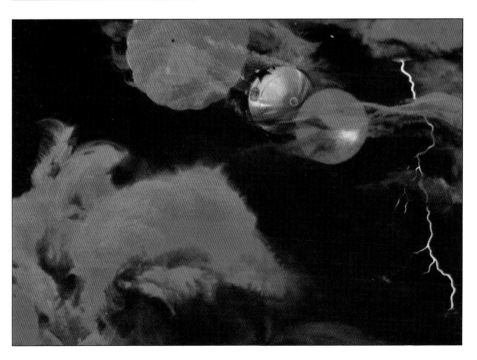

WHERE IS THE OLYMPUS MONS?

Mars is the only planet whose surface can be seen in detail from the Earth. Mars has one of the most striking surfaces of any planet in the solar system. Giant volcanoes tower above the landscape. The largest of these is the Olympus Mons, which is 25 km (15.5 miles) high, three times higher than Mount Everest. As well as this, Mars is home to Valles Marineris, a canyon that is 180 km (112 miles) wide, up to 7 km (4.3 miles) deep and long enough to stretch right across the United States of America.

Mars does not have water on its surface now, but there is evidence to show that there were rivers and seas on Mars in the past. Probes have taken many pictures of the planet's surface and scientists have identified several channels that could only have been formed by running water. Astronomers believe that there was a great deal of liquid water on Mars billions of years ago.

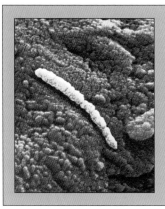

FACT FILE

In 1996 scientists produced evidence that they claimed showed living creatures inhabited Mars more than 3.6 billion years ago.

WHERE DO WE SEE METEOR SHOWERS?

The Earth meets a number of trails or clusters of tiny meteoroids at certain times every year. At such times, the sky seems filled with

a shower of sparks. Streams and swarms have orbits like those of comets and are believed to be fragments of comets.

The most brilliant meteor shower known took place on November 12–13, 1833. It was one of the Leonid showers, which occur every November and seem to come from the direction of the constellation Leo.

FACT FILE

Barringer Crater is a huge depression in the Earth in north-central Arizona. It measures about 1,275 m (4,180 ft) wide and 175 m (570 ft) deep. It was formed about 50,000 years ago when a meteorite struck the Earth.

WHERE IS THE HUBBLE TELESCOPE IN ORBIT?

The Hubble Space Telescope is a powerful telescope orbiting 610 km (380 miles) above the Earth, that provides sharper images of heavenly bodies than other telescopes. It is a reflecting telescope with a light-gathering mirror 240 cm (94 inches) in diameter. The telescope is named after American astronomer Edwin P. Hubble, who made important contributions to astronomy in the 1920s. The Hubble Space Telescope views the heavens without looking through the Earth's atmosphere. The atmosphere bends light due to a phenomenon known as diffraction, and the atmosphere is constantly moving. This combination of diffraction and movement causes starlight to jiggle about as it passes through the air, and so stars appear to twinkle.

FACT FILE

Radio observatories have radio telescopes for the study of radio waves. Most radio telescopes use large antennae to capture radio waves from space. In most cases, computers guide the telescopes and analyze the data they collect.

WHERE WAS THE FIRST COMET IMPACT OBSERVED?

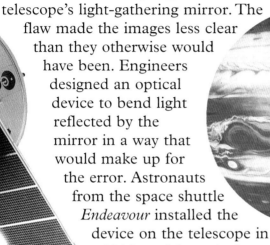

The space shuttle *Discovery* launched the telescope into orbit in 1990. Soon after launch, engineers discovered a flaw in the telescope's light-gathering mirror. The flaw made the images less clear than they otherwise would have been. Engineers designed an optical device to bend light reflected by the mirror in a way that would make up for the error. Astronauts from the space shuttle *Endeavour* installed the device on the telescope in 1993, and it worked as planned.

Along with many other telescopes, the Hubble Space Telescope observed the bombardment of Jupiter by fragments of comet Shoemaker-Levy 9 in 1994. The images showed astonishing holes in Jupiter's atmosphere where the comet pieces smashed through. This bombardment was the first comet impact ever observed when it happened.

FACT FILE

The Viking probe visited Mars in 1976 in search of life. They conducted numerous tests on Martian soils but found no evidence of any living organisms.

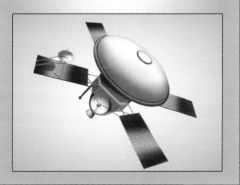

WHERE IS NASA LOCATED?

The National Aeronautics and Space Administration (NASA) is located on Merritt Island, across from a point of land called Cape Canaveral. People often call it Cape Canaveral because it was formerly located there.

NASA tests, repairs and launches space shuttles at Kennedy Space Center. To prepare a shuttle for launch, workers in the 52-storey Vehicle Assembly Building attach the external fuel tank to the orbiter (the craft that carries the crew) and two booster rockets. A huge tractor-like machine called a crawler then carries the shuttle to one of two launch pads.

FACT FILE

With the help of robots and special equipment, astronauts are able to carry out difficult repairs on satellites and space stations.

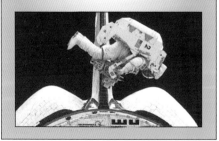

WHERE DO ASTRONAUTS DO THEIR TRAINING?

NASA astronauts do their mission training in a variety of places, including in high-flying aircraft to learn how to cope with weightlessness, and in water tanks in the 'Neutral Buoyancy Facility' to learn how to move in their bulky space suits. Most of the facilities are at the Johnson Space Center in Houston, Texas.

Astronauts preparing to stay on the International Space Station also train at the Russian Yuri Gagarin Cosmonaut Training Centre (Star City) outside Moscow, which is named after the first human being in space.

FACT FILE

NASA has sophisticated simulators that can reproduce any aspect of a mission on a craft such as the Space Shuttle. Pilots can spend time learning how to manoeuvre the craft while others can learn how to operate the other instruments.